──────────── ∽ ────────────

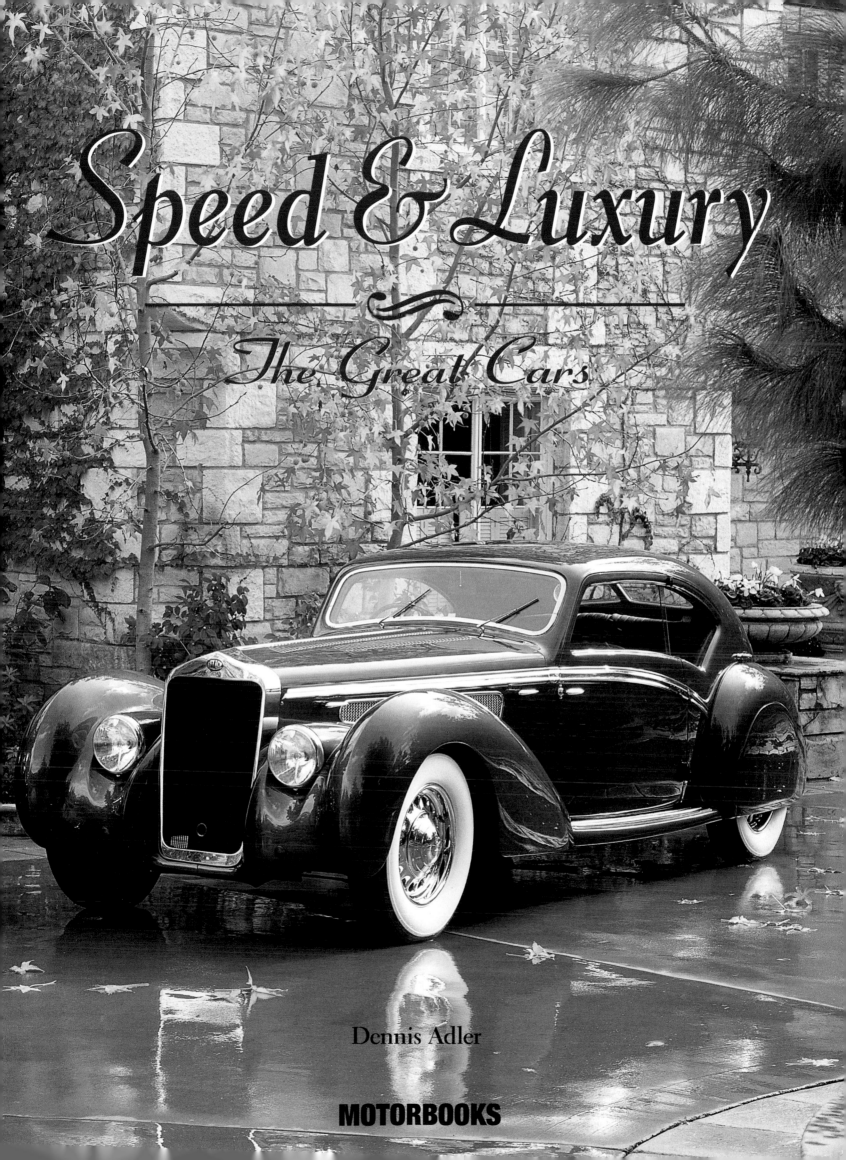

# Speed & Luxury

## The Great Cars

Dennis Adler

**MOTORBOOKS**

First published in 1997. This edition published in 2007 Motorbooks, an imprint of MBI Publishing Company, Galtier Plaza, Suite 200, 380 Jackson Street, St. Paul, MN 55101-3885 USA

Motorbooks titles are also available at discounts in bulk quantity for industrial or sales-promotional use. For details write to Special Sales Manager at MBI Publishing Company, Galtier Plaza, Suite 200, 380 Jackson Street, St. Paul, MN 55101-3885 USA.

To find out more about our books, join us online at www.motorbooks.com.

Library of Congress Cataloging-in-Publication Data

Speed & luxury : the great cars / Dennis Adler.

ISBN-10: 978-0-7603-2960-3

ISBN-10: 0-7603-0486-6 (hardcover : alk. paper)

1. Automobiles—History. 2. Automobiles—Collectors and collecting.

TL15 .A35 1997

629.222 21

97020671

Printed in China

**On the cover:**
The Type 51 Bugattis were swift cars suited to virtually any type of road competition. Beneath the hood was one of the most powerful inline eight-cylinder engines of the 1930s, a supercharged 2.3-liter (136.5-cubic-inch) dual overhead cam motor capable of developing 180 horsepower. The body on this example from The Nethercutt Collection is a one-off design by Carrossier Louis Dubos of Paris.

**On the frontispiece:** The proud rolls-Royce Spirit of Ecstasy mascot was the most recognized symbol of automotive quality in the 1920s.

**On the title pages:** The epitome of speed and luxury in 1938. The Delage D8.120 Aero Coupé and Delta Sport Cabriolet were produced for the French government by carrossier Letourneur et Marchand for display at the 1939 New York World's Fair. From the collection of Henry Uihlein, II.

**On the back cover:**
This 1935 Special Roadster, also referred to as a Sport Roadster, was built on the 500K chassis. This is believed to be the sixth 500K Special Roadster bodied at Sindelfingen.

# Contents

# Acknowledgments

———✥———

Think of this book as a life's work. Not necessarily my life's work, but the lives of Gordon Buehrig, Frank Hershey, Walter P. Chrysler, Fred and Augie Duesenberg, E.L. Cord, Howard Marmon, and a hundred others who pioneered the automobile during the classic era. Anyone who picks up this book is likely to be an automotive enthusiast and even more likely to recognize many of the cars pictured. But what few people realize at first glance is that this book, or any automotive history book, is about more than automobiles.

Since the first automotive pioneers conceived of combining a carriage with an engine more than a century ago, the history of the automobile has been about people and countries, wars and economic chaos, achievements and failures. The automobile has been there through it all and has become an inseparable part of the history of the world since 1886.

In *Speed & Luxury*, we are only looking at a small segment of that history; the finest automobiles produced from 1910 to 1948. Yet even in this narrow view, the reader will encounter many of the events which have shaped our history and culture, and the people through whose inventions, designs, and desires the automotive industry has become part of our international infrastructure. The automobile is that important.

Most histories are based on the opinions of biographers who interpret the facts through research, artifacts, and written accounts of an era. *Speed & Luxury* is no different, with the exception that the automobile is a far more tangible subject, nearly all of the cars featured in this book still exist. For that, an equal debt is owed to those who have preserved these treasures for the future, perhaps even more than to the men and women who created them in the first place.

Early car collectors like D. Cameron Peck, M.L. Bud Cohn, J.B. Nethercutt, and Bill Harrah, to name but a few, had the foresight to recognize the importance of these once-great cars decades before it become a popular hobby. Through their efforts, many of the world's most significant automobiles were preserved, a good many of which are featured in this book in their latest restored forms.

Today, collectors like Noel and Jean Thompson, Don Williams and Ken Behring, Robert M. Lee, Jim Hull and Peter Mullin, Jerry and Jean Moore, Bob Bahre, Jacques Harguindeguy, William Lyon, Jerome Sauls, Miles Collier, Arturo Keller, Joseph Murphy and Katherine Murphy, and countless others across the country and around the world are continuing the cause of preserving the past through the restoration of antique, vintage, and classic automobiles. To each of them, and the owners of the cars pictured in this book, a debt of gratitude is owed beyond that of mere words. This book is a tribute to their efforts and to the efforts of those who will follow them in the future.

*Dennis A. Adler*

# Chapter One

# Coachbuilt Luxury

## The Early Years of the Coachbuilde's Craft

$\mathcal{T}$he automobile was an idea, a vision that sprang from the inventive minds of late nineteenth century bicycle makers and engine builders, but it was German inventor Carl Benz who put all the pieces together and actually made the idea work, receiving a patent for the first motor-driven carriage in 1886.

By 1896, Americans Charles and J. Frank Duryea had received a similar patent and commenced production of the first automobiles built in the United States. That, however, is stretching things a bit. Even though the Duryea Motor Wagon Co. was the first in this country to build automobiles in series—an initial production run of 13 identical horseless carriages—there were hundreds of blacksmiths and wagon makers across the land with kerosene lanterns burning well into the night, cobbling together their own versions of the automobile. A handful of visionaries in the late 1800s were already experimenting with electric motors as an alternative power source, while others were harnessing steam to drive the wheels of progress.

By the turn of the century, encouraging breakthroughs had been made in the development of motorized transportation

---

*Steam engines had powered locomotives since the early 1800s, and a steam-powered road carriage was actually built in 1769 by Frenchman N.J. Cugnot, but it was the Stanley brothers, Francis and Frelan, of Newton, Massachusetts, who put steam power to work in a practical automotive design in 1898. By the early 1900s, models like this 1906 Stanley Steamer from the John McMullen collection numbered in the thousands, and steam had become a viable alternative to the internal combustion engine.*

*The Stanley lacked nothing in comparison to conventional automobiles other than a longer and more difficult starting process which required heating the boiler for about 20 minutes before getting underway. The cars were luxuriously appointed and by the 1920s, looked identical to gasoline-powered automobiles. The steamers were finally run off the road in 1927, when the company's new owners, Steam Vehicle Corporation of America, gave in to the car's insurmountable mechanical disadvantages over the internal combustion engine.*

*A Stanley with a full head of steam made an impressive sound, like a small locomotive, and steam power from the boiler could propel the cars to equally impressive speeds. A Stanley bodied for competition ran in the Dewar Cup at Ormond Beach, Florida, in 1907, and reached a speed of well over 150 miles per hour before crashing. Although the car was destroyed, driver Fred Marriott survived.*

———————————

using all three means of power—gasoline, electricity, and steam. To most people in 1900, however, the idea of driving, let alone owning a motorized vehicle, was a pure flight of fancy.

More than half of the world's population lived in rural areas and on farms where the horse-drawn carriage, open buggy, or merely a saddled horse was considered roadworthy transportation. And as for roads, pavement was rare even in major cities, although in Europe, paved roadways had been in use since 1816, when Briton John MacAdam originated crushed stone (macadam) pavement. He later added tar to the surface, binding the stones together to form Tarmac, still in use to this day as the most common road surface in the world. However, when the automobile arrived, the majority of roadways in use were still dirt trails carved out of the wilderness.

In 1903, Winton and Packard touring cars successfully made the first two transcontinental automobile trips across the United States to prove the potential abilities of the motorcar. The majority of early examples, however, were barely suitable to the roughhewn roadways of America and Europe, and most were no faster than a horse-drawn carriage. Travel by rail was still the only means by which one could commute from city to city with any great speed.

While the internal combustion engine was being developed in the early 1900s, American and European auto makers were also experimenting with electricity as an alternative power source. After the turn of the century, the streets of New York, Chicago, and many other major American cities were filled with the pervasive humming of electric cars as they moved almost silently down the boulevard. The electric car was perceived by most people as vastly superior to the stinking, vibrating, obstreperous gas-engined horseless carriage. Electrics, however, were strictly city cars, which greatly limited their appeal.

The most difficult problem with electric cars was, and still is, limited range. This was the main reason why experiments stopped in the mid-1900s, at a time when the lightness and improved performance of the combustion engine made the search for other forms of power less vital. However, if any one event spelled doom for the electric car it was the 1912 invention of the Kettering self-starter, a device which let a driver turn over an internal combustion engine with the push of a starter button. The electric car's single greatest advantage—no hand cranking—had been canceled out.

Although popular in Europe, electric cars enjoyed their greatest success in the United States, where Fred M. Kimball built the first vehicle of this type in 1888. The first series production was begun by the Electric Carriage and Wagon Company of Philadelphia, which supplied New York City with electric taxis in 1897. Studebaker electric cars appeared in 1902, and by 1912, there were over 20,000 electric vehicles traveling American roads.

In the early years of the American automotive industry, electric cars were produced by companies that had no previous ties to the automotive trade. For example, the Baker Motor Vehicle Co. was formed in 1898 by Walter C. Baker, president of the Cleveland-based American Ball Bearing Company. The president of Baker was Rollin H. White of the White Sewing Machine Co., who later became famous as the maker of White trucks. Baker's first car, a light two-seat electric buggy, was purchased by none other than Thomas Edison, who, when asked if he thought the automobile of the future would be an electric, replied, "I don't think so... It would be more likely that they will run by gasoline."

The most successful and longest-lived manufacturer of electric cars in America was Detroit Electric. The founding company, Anderson Carriage Manufacturing, was one of the largest carriage makers in the country, turning out as many as 15,000 horse-drawn coaches a year. In 1907, the Anderson factory in Detroit was reorganized to manufacture Detroit Electric vehicles. Noted for their very manageable steering system and instant start-up, they became especially popular with women, making a Detroit Electric the smart thing in which to be seen driving around town.

Interiors were stylishly upholstered, and seating in models such as the Brougham resembled a small sitting room, with a plush settee on one side and two smaller seats across from the driver. The coachwork was basically carriage-like in design.

During the era of the electric car, Anderson was the largest auto maker of its kind in the world, and its cars the most popular. An advertisement in 1911 stated that 14 makers of petrol-engined cars also owned Detroits. Even Henry Ford had a Detroit Electric, as did

How far have we come? In the early 1900s, electric cars like this 1918 Detroit Electric Model 75 were efficiently moving through cities at speeds up to 45 miles per hour with a range of almost 90 miles between charges. Today's latest electric cars can barely do better. An electric car was the first automobile to exceed 60 miles per hour back in 1898 with famed Belgian race driver Camille "Red Devil" Jenatzy at the wheel.

The Detroit Electric Brougham seated four, two on a large bench seat and two in small, plush chairs. The driver sat in the left rear of the compartment. Driving the Electric wasn't much different than piloting today's golf carts. A floor pedal under the driver's seat was used to select forward or reverse. The driver had two levers with which to operate steering and gear change, although the Detroit had no actual gears. Instead, each increment in the four speed motor increased electric power to hasten the car's pace, and all four speeds worked in either forward or reverse. Both the tiller steering arm and shifter folded out of the way for easier entry and exit. Across from the driver were two brake pedals, the one on the right serving as an emergency brake, operated by pressing it down and into a locked position, much the same as one would lock a golf cart emergency brake today.

Thomas Edison and Charles Edison, whose nickel-steel batteries were available at extra cost on Detroit Electrics.

Sales of Detroit Electrics, and electric vehicles in general, began to decline after World War I. In 1919, the company was renamed the Detroit Electric Car Co. Commercial Detroits ceased production in 1927, but cars continued to be built to special order. Town carriage styling similar to the 1910 pattern was still being offered as late as 1930. Very few were made after 1935, and four years later, with demand for electric vehicles almost nil, the firm closed its doors.

From the 1890s through the 1930s there were more than 300 different electric car makes in the United States alone. But what began as one of the world's most successful new industries after the turn of the century went out like a light in 1939.

*The American Underslung was a radical departure from the canons of conventional automotive engineering in the early 1900s. The main frame, instead of being carried above the axles, was hung below them on half-elliptic springs, thus lowering the overall height of the car along with its center of gravity, resulting in improved handling. Models like this 1914 Model 56 Touring from the Merle Norman collection were considered among the sportiest cars on the road. Company literature in 1913 proclaimed the Underslung, "America's Most Luxurious Car." This was one of the very last to be built.*

Motorcars had to carve their way through dust, mud, and snow on tall, spindly pneumatic tires that bogged down as easily as the wheels of a Conestoga wagon.

Throughout the first decade of the twentieth century, auto makers, both in the United States and abroad, pressed on regardless of road conditions, continually improving their designs, the performance of the internal combustion engine, and the overall practicality of the motorcar.

By 1910, the automobile was transforming the American and European landscape and the way in which people conducted their business and personal lives. Thanks to the automobile, people were no longer confined to their towns, and travel that was once measured in days, even weeks by horse-drawn carriage, was now compressed into hours and miles. The speed with which one once traveled by rail was now at the disposal of the automobilist.

Much of the motorcar's early success can be attributed to a handful of visionaries who steadfastly pursued the development of the automobile, and paramount among them was American industrialist Henry Ford. In 1896, Ford built his first motor-driven

quadricycle. After one failed attempt at the automaking business with the Henry Ford Company, he founded the Ford Motor Company in 1903.

While Ford's early models were good cars, they were neither inexpensive, nor produced in great numbers. Then in 1909, Ford changed the course of automotive history with the introduction of the Model T. By 1924, his innovative moving assembly line was producing almost half the cars in America; 1,600 Model T Fords a day, selling for as little as $490. The Model T had become the most popular and affordable automobile in the country, but it had also become an *everyman's car*, leaving the market wide open for more costly and stylish *voiture*.

In 1901, Henry Martyn Leland was contracted to produce engines for auto maker, Ransom Eli Olds. The long-established firm of Leland, Faulconer and Norton supplied 2,000 engines for the curved-dash Oldsmobile, America's first mass-produced automobile. The following year, Leland became part of the Henry Ford Company, (Ford having been asked to resign in 1901 by his partners) and on August 22, 1902, the business was reorganized as the

Cadillac Automobile Company, a name chosen in honor of Le Sieur Antoine de la Mothe Cadillac, the French explorer who had founded Detroit in the early eighteenth century.

Leland supplied engines, transmissions, and steering gears for the new Detroit-built cars and was granted a small block of stock and appointed company director. With Henry Leland at the helm, the first Cadillac automobile was completed on October 17, 1902.

Owing much to Leland's fetish for thousandths-of-an-inch accuracy, a trait rooted to his years with Connecticut firearms manufacturer Samuel Colt, Cadillac became the best-built car produced in America. In 1908 Cadillac was awarded the coveted British Dewar Trophy for engineering excellence. To achieve this distinction, three Model K Cadillacs were torn completely down, their parts mixed, and the cars reassembled under the scrutiny of the Royal Automobile Club of Great Britain. Not only did the trio of Cadillacs go back together without any filing or hand-fitting, they were immediately sent off on a 500-mile endurance run on the Brooklands track, where they ran at full throttle without a single mechanical failure!

By 1910, a Cadillac was considered one of the most prestigious automobiles in the world. In the same year, Cadillac, following Buick, Oakland, and Oldsmobile, had become part of William C. Durant's General Motors conglomerate. This gave Durant four of the most distinguished names in the American automotive industry. In 1917, after a dispute with Durant over building Liberty aircraft engines for the war effort, which Durant opposed, Henry Leland and his son Wilfred resigned their positions with Cadillac and established their own company under the name of Lincoln, the elder Leland's boyhood hero. After the war, and the production of more than 6,500 Liberty aircraft engines, the Lelands went back into the automobile business establishing the Lincoln Motor Car Company of Michigan.

In the early years of the American automotive industry, the manufacturing of luxury cars was almost a national passion. The name *American* was adopted by more auto makers in the early 1900s than any other. It was used in the incorporation of more than 45 companies between 1896 and the 1920s, but very few ever produced an automobile and others were American divisions of foreign makes, such as American Mercedes, American Fiat, and American Mors of France. The most successful American, however, was the American Motors Company (not to be confused with AMC of the 1950s) of Indianapolis, Indiana, manufacturer of the Underslung.

Known as "A Car for the Discriminating Few," the American was priced at over $4,000 in 1911 and was regarded as one of the most luxurious and expensive automobiles of the era.

The Underslung, designed by Fred Tone, who had come to American from the Marion Motor Car Company in Indianapolis, was introduced in 1907 as a roadster model and priced at $3,250. In several automotive histories, Harry Stutz has been credited with creating the novel design, but Stutz had already left the American Motors Company by 1907. Ironically, he took Tone's job at Marion! Stutz had, however, designed the conventional-chassis American models introduced in 1906.

Although some 45,000 cars were sold from 1907 to 1913, by that time the American Motors Company was virtually bankrupt. Having spent a considerable amount on expansion and improvements to the 1912 model line, American suffered tremendous financial losses due to the severe winter of 1912–1913, followed by a late spring and heavy flooding which made it almost impossible

*American Underslung owners had at their control a 50-horsepower engine, one of the most powerful available at the time, electric starting, and one of the easiest-to-control automobiles on the road. With luxurious upholstery and fastidious attention to every detail of construction, this was truly one of the greatest cars produced in the early 1900s.*

for American to deliver cars. With little cash on hand and a serious crimp in sales, the company teetered on the brink of receivership, which was brought on by concerned creditors late in 1913. When American shuttered its doors, there were 50 unsold 1914 cars in inventory, divided between the $4,000 Underslung Roadsters and Tourers and the lower-priced American Scout. The remaining cars were sold off by the Auto Parts Company of Chicago for a mere $900 apiece!

The automotive industry emerged from so many divergent fields of endeavor that at times it is almost impossible to establish a connection. While some were related in one form or another—carriage makers, engineers, industrialists—others had no apparent ties whatsoever. For example, what could have prompted a successful manufacturer of incandescent lamps and transformers to enter the automotive arena? For James Ward Packard, it was a dispute over the quality of a Winton motorcar he purchased in 1898. He felt that the automobile was deficient in some areas and when he conferred with Alexander Winton, the feisty Scotsman suggested that if Mr. Packard thought he could do a better job perhaps he should try it. Packard did, and in 1899, along with his brother William, produced his first motorcar, the Model A. By 1900, Packard had refined the design, and introduced the Model B. That year the company sold 49 cars, including two to William D. Rockefeller, a former Winton owner!

In 1904, Packard introduced its first contemporarily styled motorcar, the Model L, and the distinctive Packard radiator shell that would become a trademark for decades. A year later, the Model N added an enclosed limousine as elegant as any from Cadillac, Peerless, or Pierce-Arrow. With each successive year, Packard raised the standards of its automobiles, improving design, construction, and engineering. By 1912, when the Model Thirty Touring was introduced, Packard had become one of the most expensive automobiles sold in America, with an average price of $5,000.

*A speedometer was one of the newer features in motoring. This 1910 Packard was equipped with a patented Stewart speedometer/odometer manufactured by Stewart and Clark in Chicago.*

Late in 1915, Packard stunned the automotive industry with the Twin Six, the first 12-cylinder car put into series production anywhere in the world. Designed by Packard's new chief engineer, Jesse Vincent, who joined the firm in 1912, the Twin Six so improved production techniques that the cars sold for less than the previous six-cylinder models, with a base price starting at only $2,750 for the short 125-inch wheelbase five-passenger phaeton. Packard had not only built a more refined and more powerful car, but had built it for less. The Twin Six remained in production until 1923, by which time Packard had sold 35,000 12-cylinder automobiles, establishing itself as one of the world's leading manufacturers of luxury cars.

European auto makers, particularly those in France, Germany, and Great Britain, had a 10-year jump on American manufacturers. In Europe the automobile had become an accepted, if not preferred means of transportation by 1910. The number of European auto makers that rose to the occasion after the turn of the century could fill a book, but none stands out more than Daimler and Benz, Germany's earliest and most successful automobile manufacturers. Independent of each other until 1926, Benz and Daimler pioneered the early era of speed and luxury.

The automobile, both here and abroad, has become one of modern man's preeminent obsessions, one of the few objects that we assume to be extensions of our own personality. Like a bespoke suit or a lavish home, an automobile makes a statement about its owner. In the early years of the automotive trade, a car also made a statement about its builder, and for as long as there have been automobiles, there have been Daimler, Benz, and Mercedes-Benz models on the road.

On January 29, 1886, Carl Benz was granted a German patent for his three-wheeled, motor-driven tricycle. That summer Benz drove the prototype on a public road for the first time, just 100 meters before ending the trial, with his son Eugene running alongside the rumbling three-wheeler carrying a bottle of gasoline to fuel the engine. Benz had invented the single-cylinder motor, even the sparking plug to fire it, but he had not yet invented the gas tank!

In the town of Cannstatt, some 60 miles from Benz, another engineer by the name of Gottlieb Daimler had received a patent for

*The electric light was still on the drawing board in 1910, and Packards were equipped with attractive lantern cowl lamps. Headlights used acetylene gas, produced by combining water and calcium carbide in a separate tank mounted on the running board.*

an internal combustion engine, and with his associate Wilhelm Maybach, started construction of a four-wheeled motorized carriage. The Daimler *Motorenwagen* was introduced at virtually the same time as the Benz three-wheeler.

Benz produced around 25 three-wheeled vehicles between 1888 and 1892; the year that Benz & Co. of Mannheim introduced its first four-wheeled model, the Viktoria. Throughout the 1890s, the Mannheim factory built a variety of Viktoria-based motorcars, a design that Carl Benz saw little need to change.

By virtue of an obstinate nature, Benz had become his own worst enemy, failing to regard his early designs merely as stepping stones, the same error Henry Ford would make decades later by refusing to replace the Model T until the car was rendered virtually obsolete by his competitors. However, from his perspective, Carl Benz saw little reason to make changes. His stationary engine business was booming and by the late 1890s Benz & Co. was the largest manufacturer of motorcars in the world. What Benz needed most was to invent the rearview mirror, so that he could see how close Daimler was to running him off the road by 1901.

*It was referred to as a gentleman's car built by gentlemen. This 1910 Packard Model Eighteen Touring, from the Classic Car Club of America Museum, is a prime example of the luxurious styling which helped establish Packard in the early 1900s.*

During this same period, Daimler Motoren Gessellschaft developed and patented the first V-twin engine, a four-speed gearbox with gated linkage, a jet-type carburetor (still the basis for modern carburetors), and the first motorcar with a front-mounted engine—a significant step beyond the limited styling of the Benz and early Daimler models, which had euphemistically put the cart before the horse.

In 1901, Daimler introduced the Mercedes, designed by Paul Daimler and Wilhelm Maybach, and named after the daughter of financier and company board member Emil Jellinek. The Mercedes would become the first modern motorcar, the foundation upon which every successful automobile has since been based. With one bold stroke in 1901, Daimler Motoren Gessellschaft rendered virtually obsolete every motorcar created up to that moment.

The popularity of Benz and Daimler automobiles had already spread to this country by the turn of the century, in part through the efforts of William Steinway, the successful New York piano manufacturer. While visiting Europe in 1888, he learned of Daimler's work and went to see this fantastic invention for himself. Steinway was so taken with the idea of motorized transportation that he secured patent rights to Daimler's engines and vehicles so he could build them in the United States. He set up the Daimler Motor Company in Hartford, Connecticut, to produce engines, but decided not to build any cars because American roads were still unsuitable for automotive travel. When Steinway died in 1896, the company was reorganized as Daimler Manufacturing Company of Long Island City, continuing to produce engines while adding a line of motor launches, a few commercial vehicles, and importing Daimler auto-

Early designs, regardless of coachwork, had the gear change and hand brake mounted outside of the driving compartment, and mounted through the frame rail to the transmission.

In the early 1900s, Mercedes styling ran the gamut from conservative formal limousines and landaulettes to dashing phaetons and high-spirited sport two-seaters. None, however, approached the styling of the one-off 1911 Labourdette Skiff, the most exotic non-racing Mercedes built prior to World War I.

The Avenue des Champs-Elysées atelier of Henri Labourdette pioneered the exquisite wooden skiff torpedo design in 1910, a body style which would became popular in Europe during the early 1920s.

We might marvel at these cars today and wonder how a single body could have justified so much work—the hundreds of individual hand-cut strips of mahogany and thousands of copper nails used to attach the planks to the body's hand-built wooden framework. In 1911, people were no doubt equally compelled to express wonderment when this 37/90-horse-

This 1911 Labourdette Skiff, from the B. Scott Isquick collection, built on a Mercedes Model 90-horsepower chassis, is easily the most exotic non-racing Mercedes built prior to World War I. The triple-layer body was created by criss-crossing tiers of mahogany over a ribbed frame, then applying a third horizontal layer atop the substructure. It required 2,700 brass rivets to attach the exterior plies.

power Mercedes chassis appeared, the only known example of a Labourdette Skiff ever mounted to a Mercedes running gear. (In 1921 a mahogany-bodied boattail was built on a 28/95-horsepower chassis, but not by Labourdette.)

The majority of Labourdette Skiff bodies had been built by the mid-1920s, mainly on French chassis such as Panhard & Levassor, Peugeot, and Delaunay-Belleville. One of the few "foreign" chassis to be fitted with Skiff coachwork was a 1913 Rolls-Royce, bodied as a dual windshield torpedo and almost identical in design to the 1911 Mercedes. A similar body was also mounted on a 1914 Panhard & Levassor chassis. Additionally, Labourdette bodied a 1913 Mercedes chassis (possibly a Mercedes-Knight) as a limousine-phaeton with traditional panel-beaten coachwork and a 1928 SS in a rakish sport roadster body with rumble seat.

The 1911 Mercedes 37/90-horsepower chassis was delivered to the atelier at 35 Avenue des Champs-Elysées, Paris in 1911, on behalf of the car's owner, American hat maker Henry G. Stetson. The completed Skiff was delivered to Stetson's Elkins Park residence outside Philadelphia in 1912 through the Mercedes dealer in New York City. The car cost Stetson an incredible $18,000.

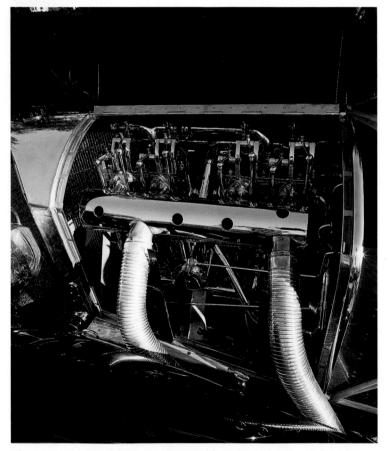

The Mercedes Model 90 was powered by a huge 9.5-liter inline four-cylinder engine. The motor was comprised of two blocks of two cylinders, with the valvetrains in each controlled by a single cam located high in the crankcase. Producing 90 horsepower at 1,300 rpm, the engine was one of the most advanced designs in the world, utilizing three overhead poppet-type valves per cylinder. Fuel delivery was by a single-barrel, sliding-piston carburetor.

*The Victoria Touring body of this 1911 Benz, designed by A.T. Demarest & Co. of New York City, features a large rear tonneau with folding top; a removable canvas hood covers the driver's compartment. The car has neither windows nor side curtains, consigning it strictly to fair weather driving.*

---

mobiles. With the advent of the Mercedes, the Steinway company decided to get into vehicle manufacturing and in 1905 began production of the American Mercedes, an exact duplicate of the 45-horsepower model which had become the rage of Europe.

Well on its way to becoming one of the most prestigious cars manufactured in the United States, a disastrous fire razed the entire Long Island City factory in February 1907, bringing an end to the American-made Mercedes.

One of the most exciting German cars of the early 1900s was the Mercedes. Beginning in 1910, the most powerful model was the 37/90-horsepower chassis produced through 1914, and replaced the following year by a larger-displacement 38/100-horsepower model. The 90-horsepower was powered by a four-cylinder engine with a bore and stroke of 130x180 millimeters (5x7 inches), displacing 9,530 cubic centimeters (approximately 400 cubic inches) and delivering 90 brake horsepower at 1,300 rpm. The inline engine had two blocks of two cylinders each with three overhead valves per cylinder and a single camshaft mounted high in the crankcase. Fuel delivery was through a single Mercedes sliding-piston carburetor. A four-speed gearbox, with a gate change shifter mounted outside the body, delivered the engine's *puissance* to a

chain-driven rear axle. Daimler Motoren Gesellschaft estimated the average top speed for the cars at 115 kilometers per hour—roughly 70 miles per hour—although it was reported that with lightweight coachwork they could reach almost 100 miles per hour.

In addition to Mercedes, Benz was among the best-known imports throughout the early 1900s. Benz established an American distributorship in New York City with representatives in Philadelphia, Atlanta, and Chicago.

For 1911, Benz chassis prices ranged from $3,250 for the 18-horsepower model up to a stunning $8,500 for the sporty 60-horsepower versions. Mind you, a new Model T Ford sold for only $900 in 1911, and that was a complete car, not a bare chassis! Except for the 60-horsepower models, bodied mainly as sport runabouts, the 45-horsepower Benz was the top of the line, offering the greatest variety of custom and standard coachwork, with normal body prices from $1,000 to $2,250.

In France, Renault, one of the oldest auto makers in Europe, opened its doors in 1899.

While Daimler is often credited with producing the first front-engined automobile in 1900, Renault actually introduced its 1-3/4-horsepower buggy with front-mounted engine, shaft drive, and a

All early Benz motors had cylinders cast in pairs, with those of small displacement having all their valves on one side and operated from a single camshaft. Larger displacement engines, such as this 50-horsepower example, used a dual T-head design with two camshafts, one on the induction side, another on the exhaust side. The 50-horsepower model had a top speed of 90 kilometers per hour (56 miles per hour).

The driving compartment of this 1911 Benz is both spacious and beautifully decorated with polished mahogany and leather trim. At the base of the steering column, a small foot throttle is surrounded by three larger pedals. There are two foot brakes, one on the extreme left, another on the extreme right, acting on the drive shaft. The inside left pedal operates the clutch.

A rare piece of Detroit history, this 1917 Detroiter five-passenger Touring is the last known example equipped with the six-cylinder Continental engine. Owner Loyal Jodar notes that the Detroiter Motor Car Company produced these cars almost entirely from outsourced components. A handsome body style for the early 1900s, the Detroiter closely resembled early Dodge Brothers cars in design. Detroiter was organized in 1911 by Claude S. Briggs, former sales manager for the Brush Runabout Company, and John A. Boyle of Detroit.

*A stylish car for 1917, the Detroiter Model 6-45 Touring could accommodate five passengers. The last model year for the company, a total of five different body styles were offered: Touring, Roadster, Luxemore Roadster, Convertible Coupe, and Touring Sedan.*

As an auto maker, Renault produced cars that were affordable and practical, leaving the luxury car field to contemporaries like Bugatti, Delage, and Delahaye.

In Great Britain, there was only one word for luxury, well, actually two words, Rolls-Royce, created by the amalgamation of C.S. Rolls & Co. and Royce & Co. Ltd. in March 1906. The following year Messrs. Frederick Henry Royce and Charles Stewart Rolls introduced the Silver Ghost, so named for the 13th car produced, which featured a distinctive gray color scheme and silver-plated fitments. All succeeding 40- and 50-horsepower six-cylinder Rolls-Royce models were known as Silver Ghosts.

From the onset, Rolls-Royce automobiles set an international standard for quality, luxury, and engineering, and by 1910 the Silver Ghost was the most desirable luxury automobile in the world, a car for monarchs, potentates, and captains of industry. It remained in production until 1924.

They say that nothing is ever more exciting than when it begins. No statement could better describe the emergence of the automotive industry in the early 1900s. Although faster and more refined cars would follow, the automobile, however improved in the ensuing decades, would never again make as many advances as it did from 1900 to 1924.

three-speed gearbox one year before. With a capital investment of 40,000 francs put up by his elder brothers, Fernand and Marcel, Louis Renault established a factory on the grounds of the family home in Billancourt and with a staff of 60 workers produced 71 cars. The following year production rose to 179 cars and Renault was on the road to success as one of France's premiere auto makers.

Throughout the early years, Renault continued to advance the design of the automobile, albeit in the French idiom, disposed to his own styling ideas, particularly the unique shape of the Renault hood, which became an early trademark. By 1913, Renault was France's largest motor vehicle manufacturer with an output of more than 10,000 cars a year and a workforce of nearly 4,000 men.

During World War I, Renault produced V-8 aero engines for the Farman biplane, manufactured light tanks, and developed a V-12 aero engine which was used in the celebrated Bregurt 14 biplane fighter. Following the Armistice, Renault resumed automobile production, and expanded further into the aviation field becoming the largest aero engine manufacturer in the world by 1930.

*Although the majority of the car's components were purchased from other manufacturers, the Detroiters had a well-designed and finished appearance.*

*Typical of the reserved but elegant styling of Cadillac models in the early 1920s, this 1922 Type 61 Touring, from the Leo Brown collection, features a higher radiator and raised hood line indicative of the revised styling introduced that year on all Cadillac models.*

*It would be hard to argue the fact that European cars produced in the early 1900s were more stylish than those built in the United States. This elegant 1913 Mercedes Model 90-horsepower Touring features styling of classic proportions, an open driving compartment, and massive exhaust pipes intimating the promise of spectacular power and performance from this automobile.*

Throughout the early 1900s, the Rolls-Royce Silver Ghost was regarded as one of the best-built motor cars in the world. In 1911, Claude Goodman Johnson, a partner of Rolls and the man responsible for first naming Rolls-Royce models, came up with the advertising slogan, "The Best Car in the World." Luxury and prestige, however, were not the only attributes of the Silver Ghost. Models such as this 1913 Alpine Tourer, from the William B. Ruger, Sr. collection, were also recognized as spirited competitors in hill climbs and reliability runs.

The driver had very few distractions in the Silver Ghost. Pressure gauges were located on the firewall, and the majority of controls were off the steering wheel hub.

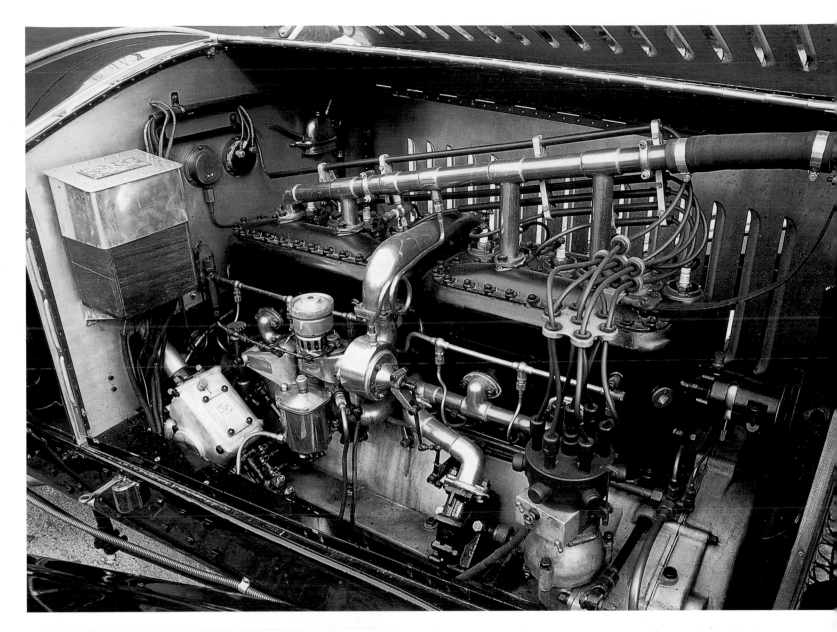

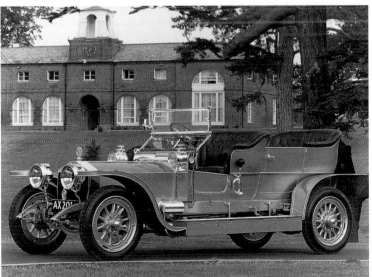

The Silver Ghost engine was cast in two blocks of three cylinders with a square bore and stroke of 114 millimeters (4-1/2 inches) displacing 7,046 cubic centimeters.

Of all the Rolls-Royce models produced over the past 93 years, none has been as significant as the first Silver Ghost, introduced in 1907. The name was chosen by RR general manager Claude Johnson, who had taken to giving the cars romantic epithets like "The Mystery." "The Silver Ghost" seemed appropriate for the new 40-50-horsepower model's gray color scheme and silver-plated fitments. The name was so well liked that afterward all subsequent chassis in the series were named "Silver Ghost." The original car is still in the possession of Rolls-Royce and in perfect running condition!

# Chapter Two

# Rumble Seats and Roadsters — Cars from 1910 to 1924

## The Sporting Car Takes to the Road

Before the turn of the century, gentlemen racers were already testing their skills and the mettle of their motorcars in sporting contests. The first major competition, a 742-mile race from Paris to Bordeaux and back to Paris, took place in 1895. It was won by French auto maker Emile Levassor, who drove the course in his massive Panhard et Levassor tonneau for nearly 48 hours at an average speed of 15 miles per hour! The following year Levassor was injured in the Paris-Marseilles race and later died from complications. The point being that this need to compete, to risk life and limb, has been in our blood since the beginning of time. In the automotive world, competition eventually boiled down to one all-encompassing design: the sports car.

How one defines a sports car depends upon the era in which it was built, and, in the early, 1900s it was built as simply as possible. Early models like the Mercer Raceabout and Stutz Bearcat were hell on wheels—hairy, thundering machines that were little more than two seats attached to a chassis and engine. It was atop cars like these that legendary race drivers Ralph DePalma, Spencer Wishart, and Barney Oldfield built their reputations.

*Racing made it great, but Barney Oldfield made the Marmon Wasp Speedster famous. Chosen as the Official Pacesetter for the eighth running of the Indianapolis Memorial Day classic, Oldfield and the 1920 Marmon stunned both spectators and race drivers by turning a sensational 80 miles per hour pace lap before pulling into the pits. Even Oldfield's legendary rival Ralph DePalma—who was on the pole that year—remarked that the Marmon may have been the fastest car on the track. Owned today by Jack Dunning, this is the actual car purchased by Oldfield in 1920.*

*The sporty Mercer Raceabout came with a monocle windshield, if one at all, a large round fuel tank consuming the rear of the body, and only enough coachwork to cover the large wooden artillery wheels and conceal the 50-horsepower four-cylinder engine.*

*Spartan in design but not lacking in features, the 1913 Mercer Raceabout came with full instrumentation and a speedometer. It was a road car that could double as a racer for the amateur sportsman.*

In 1910, the Mercer Automobile Company was established in Trenton, Mercer County, New Jersey. If Ford was building family cars and Cadillac luxury models, then Mercer was building sports cars. The company produced three models, the two-passenger Speedster (later named Raceabout), five-place Touring (with more substantial coachwork), and the Toy Tonneau four-seater. The Type 35 Raceabout was Mercer's most famous car and although not endowed with a particularly large engine, just 300 cubic inches, nor exceptional *puissance*, the T-head four, mounted to the lightweight chassis and rudimentary bodywork, proved to be quite ample. The cars were equipped with a superb three-speed selective transmission, later improved to a four-speed in 1913, and an oil-wetted multiple-disc clutch, which contributed to the two-seater's agile performance.

In 1911, Mercer Raceabouts won five out of six major races in

*This example of the Mercer Type 35 Raceabout, from the William B. Ruger, Sr. collection, is one of the earliest American sports cars. They were equipped with a superb three-speed selective transmission, later improved to a four-speed in 1913, and an oil-wetted multiple-disc clutch, which contributed to the two-seater's agile performance. The Mercer Raceabout sold for an average of $2,500 in 1913.*

which they were entered. The following year at the Los Angeles Speedway, Ralph DePalma established eight new world records with a Raceabout, and Spencer Wishart took a Model 35 off the showroom floor of an Ohio dealer and handily won a 200-mile race in Columbus, establishing four new dirt-track records in the process. In 1913, a racing model driven by Wishart finished second in the Indianapolis 500.

Advertised as "The Champion Light Car," Mercer's successful string of racing victories through 1916 established the company's image as a leader in early motorsports competition. With Mercer, less was more and the gossamer bodywork of the Raceabout was not indicative of its cost, an average of $2,500 by 1913.

The Mercer's sporty styling was not lost on the competition, principally Indianapolis auto maker Harry Stutz, whose all-new 1912 Bearcat looked remarkably similar. Independent coach-builders began offering Mercer-styled bodies to replace those of the humdrum Model T. The Raceabout look also appeared on early Oakland models, like the 1915 Type 37 Speedster, a more luxurious interpretation of the Mercer and Stutz designs.

Oakland was incorporated in Pontiac, Michigan, by Edward N. Murphy as the Pontiac Buggy Company in 1891, but had to be renamed after rival Pontiac Spring and Wagon Works introduced a motorized high-wheeler under the Pontiac name. Murphy chose the Oakland name, which he had used for his wagons, and rein-corporated in August 1907 with associate Alanson P. Brush, who was to become one of the most influential automobile engineers of the early 1900s. A bit touchy, he had promptly resigned from Cadil-lac when the company, then under the control of Henry Leland, turned down his innovative design for a vertical, counter-rotating two-cylinder engine, which he then brought to Murphy. The two formed a brief partnership which ended when Brush took off to start his own company and produce the single-cylinder Brush Run-about with Frank Briscoe.

Brush left Murphy with a somewhat unsuccessful car on his hands, which he decided to change in 1909 by dropping the Brush-designed two-cylinder engine in favor of a conventional 40-horse-power four. Well on the road to success, and having just concluded the sale of Oakland to William C. Durant, Murphy died at the age of 44.

*The Oakland's interior was simple but elegantly trimmed with nickel-plated instruments, gear selector, and hand brake. The cars featured a Stewart drum-type speedometer, odometer, and trip meter.*

*As a true sporting car, the Oakland Speedster had no doors. One simply stepped on the running boards and over the short body panels.*

Once in the GM fold, Oakland quickly began to prosper. The four-cylinder line, consisting of roadster and touring models, became one of GM's best sellers, with as many as 5,000 cars a year being delivered.

By 1913, the Oakland had increased in both size and power, now with a 130-inch wheelbase and a new 60-horsepower, 334-cubic inch six-cylinder engine. Nearly 9,000 Oaklands, featuring the Kettering self-starter and electric lights, were sold in 1913. Within two years, sales were approaching 1,000 cars per month and that figure doubled by 1916, when an eight-cylinder engine was added.

The sporty, lightweight styling of the Mercer Raceabout and Stutz Bearcat inspired a number of American auto makers to produce purebred road racers, but few improved upon the design with the gentility of Oakland. The 1915 Model 37 Speedster captured the essence of the brutish two-seaters, but tempered it with extraordinary grace and character, giving up nothing to either Stutz or

*The sporty styling of the Mercer and Stutz inspired a number of American automakers, but few improved upon the design with the gentility of Oakland. The 1915 Model 37 Speedster captured the essence of the brutish road racers tempering it with extraordinary grace, yet giving up nothing to either Stutz or Mercer. Oaklands, like this rare example from the John McMullen collection, performed admirably in motor sport competition, particularly reliability runs and hill climbs, winning no less than 25 of the latter.*

*Need to check the fuel gauge? You got out and walked back to the gas tank. The gauge was a true convenience; on most cars one had to open the cap and measure the fuel level with a stick.*

Mercer. Oaklands performed admirably in motor sport competition, and particularly in reliability runs and hill climbs, winning no less than 25 of the latter by 1916.

Basically a Spartan design, the Speedster body, added to the Oakland model line in 1915 and continuing through 1916, had no provision for a trunk, and was supplied with dual spares fitted to the flat rear deck. As a true sporting car, the Oakland Speedster also lacked doors—one simply stepped on the running boards, over the short body panels and into the seat. The interior was simple, but elegantly trimmed with nickel-plated instruments—Stewart drum-type speedometer, odometer, and trip meter—and a plated gear selector and hand brake. Although not uncommon for the era, another item absent from the Oakland was an instrument panel fuel gauge. However, GM at least gave drivers something better than a stick to shove down the fuel filler; attached to the fuel tank at the back of the rear deck was a fuel level gauge.

Billed as "The smartest and best little car ever marketed in America at anything like the money," the 1910 Hupmobile Runabout, an 1,100-pound featherweight, sold for only $750. The sporty little two-seater, the brainchild of Robert Craig Hupp, who launched his Detroit, Michigan, auto manufacturing company in November 1908, was powered by a 2.8-liter four-cylinder engine developing 20 horsepower. In 1910, Hupp sold 5,340 cars. This example from the Classic Car Club of America Museum is one of the few remaining.

The Hupmobile Runabout was a simple car. No gauges; just a brake, clutch, gas pedal, and steering wheel. The gear selector and hand brake were mounted through the frame to the driver's right.

The Oakland Model 37 Speedster was powered by a four-cylinder engine developing 39 horsepower, not exactly chest-swelling *puissance*, but given the weight of the body, power enough to attain better than 60 mph. At the same time, Oakland also offered the Model 49 powered by a six-cylinder engine, and the Model 50 with eight cylinders. However, the Speedster appears to have only been offered in the four-cylinder line.

Rudimentary raceabouts like the Model 37 were not long for the automotive world, as styling, engineering, and performance improvements led to faster and more-refined sports cars, including the Oakland Model 34 Roadster, which became the marque's leading sports model in 1917. By then, the era of the open-bodied Stutz, Mercer, and Oakland Speedsters was over, and maybe with it, some of the innocence and rugged adventure that made the gentlemen's sport of motor racing so exciting in those first years after the turn of the century.

Oakland remained one of GM's best-selling lines, and in 1932, became the Pontiac Motor Company Division of General Motors.

Not all great things last. More auto makers fell by the roadside than survived the first quarter-century of the automobile in America. Many were very good companies felled by bad investments. In the early 1920s, the Kissel car was one of the most advanced automobiles in the world, and the Kissel company was destined for greatness, greatness that unfortunately would never be realized.

The Kissel lived its short but productive life from 1907 to 1931, a mere 24 years, during which time the Hartford, Wisconsin, company made what we would call today, state-of-the-art automobiles.

The Kissel family, like many others in Wisconsin, had emigrated to the United States from Germany in the 1800s. By the turn of the century, L. Kissel and Sons was known for home building, real estate, and a variety of related companies, none of which had anything to do with automobiles. However, in 1905, brothers George and Will, both in their 20s, decided to build an experimental automobile. It was a four-cylinder runabout with shaft drive. Considering that the majority of automobiles in the world were still utilizing chain drive in 1905, this was a rather ambitious undertak-

*Right behind the Oakland in GM's model line-up was the Buick; the company upon which W.C. Durant had built his GM empire by 1911, when this sporty Model 26 Roadster from the CCCA Museum was introduced. The cars were equipped with a new 210-cubic inch four-cylinder engine producing 25.6 horsepower. In 1911, Buick sold 1,000 Model 26 Roadsters.*

ing. A year later, the Kissel brothers opened their own assembly plant.

Using local talent, bodies for the early cars were built by the sleigh-manufacturing Zimmermann Brothers in nearby Waupun, and engines used for the first roadsters and touring models were built by the Beaver company.

The addition of Herman Palmer as chief engineer and J. Friedreich Werner, a German coachbuilder with impeccable credentials, including a stint with Opel Motor Works in Russelsheim, rounded out the Kissel organization. By 1909, the company was offering a full line of automobiles and trucks.

In 1911, Kissel introduced the double-drop frame (with a kick-up over both front and rear wheels), and its use of three dash lamps under a steel cornice in 1914 pioneered indirect illumination of

dashboard instruments. The Kissels were also among the first American auto makers to offer wind-up windows.

The sportiest Kissel models built in the 1920s were designed in collaboration with New York distributor Conover T. Silver, and among them was a speedster known as the Gold Bug, featuring innovative outrigger seats which pulled out of a storage drawer on either side of the body. Certainly an interesting way to accommodate two additional passengers. The Kissel Speedsters and Toursters, as well as the spirited razor-edge 1922 Coach Sedan, were all popular models powered by an L-head, six-cylinder engine introduced in 1915, a design which remained in production with only minor changes through 1928.

Production of 2,123 cars in 1923 showed promise after the company had suffered declining sales throughout the postwar

One of the smartest looking cars of the early 1920s was the Kissel Gold Bug. This 1923 example from William B. Ruger's collection is one of a handful of restored Kissel speedsters left. Designed in collaboration with New York distributor Conover T. Silver, the Gold Bug featured an innovative outrigger seat that folded neatly into a drawer on each side of the body.

The Kissel speedster had a cockpit-style interior with instruments mounted on a polished metal fascia. Its clean, mechanical appearance added to the car's sporty image and popularity among Hollywood celebrities in the 1920s.

recession, but in 1924, production tumbled to 803 cars. Retooling problems for the all-new 1925 model line and introduction of the Lycoming-based Kissel straight-eight delayed new model deliveries, further straining the company coffers.

In the *Standard Catalog of American Cars 1805-1942* historian Beverly Rae Kimes aptly summarized Kissel's declining years. "The company's production figures tell the story," wrote Kimes. "[In] 1925, 2,122 units; 1926, 1,972 units; 1927, 1,147 units; 1928, 1,068 units; 1929, 881 units—and of the totals for 1928 and 1929, 200 each year were National-Kissel funeral cars to be distributed through the National Casket Company. Another ominous sign."

By 1930, Kissel would be able to drive itself to its own funeral. That was the year bank credit was shut off and the business mort-

gaged to the hilt. George Kissel nailed the coffin shut by entering into an agreement with automotive entrepreneur Archie Andrews, who promised to obtain $250,000 in new loans for the company in exchange for a commitment to build 1,500 of his new Ruxton front-drive cars. But Andrews' financial contributions stopped at $100,000. Leveraged even further and the assembly lines split between Ruxton components and their own cars, the Kissels could not continue. Rather than have their company fall into Andrews' hands, as had the Moon Motor Car Co. through similar circumstances, George Kissel requested a friendly creditor to bring on

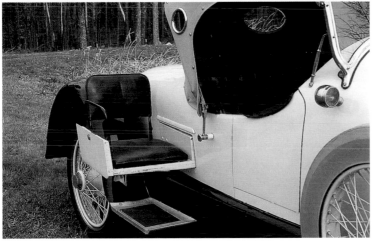

*Gold Bug was chosen from among 500 entries in a contest to name the new Kissel. The beetle-back design and bright yellow color scheme no doubt inspired someone to come up with the rather peculiar appellation.*

*It is unlikely that this idea would pass safety standards today, but in the early 1920s, the Kissel's unusual outrigger seats attracted a lot of attention. Most roadster manufacturers relied on rumble seats to accommodate additional passengers.*

receivership in September 1930. Bankruptcy was declared and the Kissels took Ruxton and Andrews down with them.

Every marque has its moment of glory. For some, it is at the beginning of their history, others in the middle, and for a few, it comes at the end. For Marmon, one of the most distinguished American cars ever produced, it was all of the above.

Howard Marmon was chief engineer of his family's milling machinery business, Nordyke and Marmon, and in 1902 he completed his first prototype automobile. Although strictly experimental, it was remarkably progressive for its time, featuring an overhead-valve air-cooled two-cylinder engine in 90-degree V configuration, a multiple disc clutch in the flywheel, three-speed selective sliding gear transmission, a subframe carrying engine and transmission with single three-point suspension, a force-feed lubrication system, and shaft drive.

The V-twin was never produced, but its successor, the 24-horsepower V-4 Model A, with aluminum front seat structure,

went into production in 1904. A total of six cars were sold, and the following year Marmon began series production of the improved Model B, powered by an air-cooled V-4. Priced at $2,500, the V-4 line was manufactured through 1909.

Having a foundry at his disposal, Marmon was able to design and manufacture special components for his cars, and soon the entire body was made of aluminum, as well as much of the running gear. In 1909, Marmon changed to a conventional inline, four-cylinder, water-cooled design, which was better suited to mass production, and from then on, all Marmons used water cooling and conventional inline T-head engines.

The most significant Marmon of the early 1900s was the Model 34 introduced by the Indianapolis, Indiana, auto maker in 1916. This was followed by the Model 34B in 1920, acclaimed as Marmon's greatest product.

Assisting with the original design was Alanson P. Brush, who seemed to play pivotal roles in the foundation of several automotive companies. The Marmon's design, which was patented by Brush in 1914, and introduced on the Model 34, incorporated the running boards, their supporting members, and the splash pans into

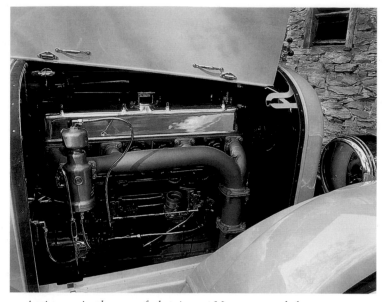

*A pioneer in the use of aluminum, Marmon used the lightweight alloy in the manufacture of the 34B engine's crankcase, cylinder head covers, timing gear case and cover, and the ring carrying the upper half of the pistons. Displacing 339.7 cubic inches, the valve-in-head six had a 3 3/4x5 1/8-inch bore and stroke and delivered 80 horsepower at 2,450 rpm, capable of propelling the Marmon to 80 miles per hour. Only the Indy 500 pacesetter and a second car for Howard Marmon were ever equipped with the dual Zenith carburetors in place of the standard Stromberg 0-2 carburetor.*

———————

the load-bearing structure. While the bare chassis was somewhat unusual in appearance, it proved to be a breakthrough in platform design, achieving both a reduction in weight and an increase in strength. The advanced design of the Model 34 series featured "unification construction," making the body and chassis nearly one—essentially an early version of unibody construction, which would not become an industry standard for decades.

Regarded as one of the best-handling cars on the road in 1916, the Model 34 had an even 50-50 front-to-rear weight distribution.

Marmon offered a variety of body styles, with open cars manufactured at the factory; limousines built by New Haven, Thompson, or Holbrook; landaulettes and town cars by New Haven and Holbrook; and convertible sedans by Thompson. The bodies for the Model 34B Speedsters were manufactured for Marmon by the Hume Body Company of Rochester, New York, and made entirely of lightweight aluminum over a braced framework of ash. Total weight of the Speedster was a mere 3,295 pounds.

The Marmon 34B Speedster was noted for its distinctive appearance and exceptional speed, quick enough, in fact, that it could indeed have been a race car. Fitted with a special 3.0:1 ratio axle, a Speedster was timed around the 2.5-mile Indianapolis Motor Speedway track at 2 minutes, 6 seconds—an average of 71 mph—for 1920, an exceptional top speed for anything that wasn't there to race. That same year, the Speedster was chosen as the Official Pacesetter for the eighth running of the Memorial Day classic, with Barney Oldfield as the driver.

Prior to the race, there had been some speculation as to whether a standard, fully equipped production car could maintain an average speed of better than 60 miles per hour, which was nec-

*Noted for their interior design, the Wasp Speedsters had controls and instruments conveniently positioned in a single cluster with indirect or "glareless" lighting. The driver's seat was positioned further back than usual, requiring a special tilted steering column and deeply dished steering wheel. The gear shift and brake were located close at hand and foot pedals positioned to allow quick movement from throttle to brake and clutch. Although the term is not applied to models of this era, the Marmon Speedster truly was "a driver's car."*

———————

essary to bring the field up to speed on the pace lap. No doubt, those who had little faith in the Marmon were chagrined when Oldfield led the starting grid around the course at a sensational 80-mile-per-hour clip before pulling off at the end of the pace lap. Even Oldfield's legendary rival Ralph DePalma—who was on the pole that year—remarked that the Marmon may have been the fastest car on the track. Oldfield was so impressed with the Speedster's performance that he purchased the car after the race. This was perhaps the single greatest endorsement Marmon could have ever received. Oldfield drove the Marmon Pacesetter coast-to-coast eight times promoting a line of tires bearing his name.

The Speedster became so popular with the public, that on August 20, 1920, Marmon announced production of a "Wasp

Speedster" in Marmon Racing Yellow, equipped with the special 3.0:1 axle (3.75:1 was standard) and a 0-100-mile-per-hour speedometer. Identical to the Indy Pacesetter, with matching wire wheels, Goodrich or Goodyear cord tires, black radiator shell, fenders, dust deflectors, running gear, and nickel-plated metal trimming, these 1921 models may well represent the first time a manufacturer offered replicas of an Indianapolis 500 Pace Car!

During the 1920s, prices for the Model 34B were cut back to improve sales and by 1923, with prices starting at only $3,185 for a touring car, nearly 3,000 Marmons were delivered. The Model 34 series was continued in production through 1924, and in refined versions, designated Models 74 and 75, sold through 1928.

In Europe, the sporting car had been a tradition since the days of Panhard et Levassor, and the first Benz and Mercedes open-wheel racers of 1903. Throughout the first half of the decade, sporting cars continued to proliferate until World War I brought an abrupt end to the production of European automobiles in 1914, particularly those built in Germany. Ironically, it was the war which led to one of Mercedes' most successful sports racing models, the 28/95 Targa Florio, which was powered by a Daimler aircraft engine.

The practice of adapting aircraft engines to fit motorcars was not unusual, but Mercedes was among the first to attempt it in the early 1900s. While modifying an aircraft engine to suit the needs of an automobile—mounting it to a chassis and linking it to a rear differential via gear-change transmission and driveshaft—was never that difficult,

*Just prior to World War I, Daimler had introduced the mightiest race car in its history, the 28/95 powered by a modified Daimler DF80 aircraft engine. Production of the 28/95 Mercedes resumed in 1920 with an improved version of the Daimler aero engine. The Mercedes chassis was a good place to put the engine, since the Treaty of Versailles prohibited Germany from producing aircraft. This 1922 Targa Florio, named after the Italian road race in which factory driver Max Sailer captured a class win in 1921, was one of seven team cars campaigned in the 1922 event, and likely driven by Christian Werner to a second-place class finish. However, since historical records are sketchy, it is possible that this supercharged model 28/95 could have been the car Sailer drove to first place in the Coppa Florio, the racing division for production-based touring cars competing in the Targa Florio.*

---

*From the time of their introduction, Mercedes 28/95 Sport models were equipped with four-wheel mechanical brakes; not until later did they appear on the long-wheelbase 28/95 chassis.*

these modifications were customarily made to engines being adapted for use in race cars, and not for passenger vehicle applications. With the 28/95 Mercedes, Daimler managed to accomplish both.

Introduced in 1914, the 28/95 Mercedes was directly inspired by the aero-engined sixes that had raced at Le Mans the previous year. Except for the necessary crankcase alterations required for an automotive installation, the 105x140-millimeter (7,250-cc) overhead cam sixes used in the 28/95 Mercedes were virtually identical to the Daimler-built DF80 aircraft engines.

Although the factory had planned an entire range of models around this engine and chassis combination in 1914, few were actually built before the war. The 28/95 was reintroduced in 1920 as one of D.M.G.'s principal postwar models, and produced in considerable numbers through 1924. Both series can be cited as good examples of how race car design influenced and improved passenger car development at D.M.G. from 1914 on.

The 28/95 chassis were originally available in two wheelbase lengths, 3,390 millimeters (133.5 inches) and 3,555 millimeters (140 inches). A 3,065-millimeter (120.6-inch) wheelbase sport chassis, designed by Paul Daimler and D.M.G. engineer and race driver Max Sailer, was added to the line in 1921.

*The Targa Florio name was applied to all 28/95 models, but those with the competition bodies were built on a special 120.6-inch sport chassis designed by Paul Daimler and Max Sailer in 1921. The Targa Florio was a massive car pared down to racing trim. Coachwork was minimal, fitted with vestigial fenders (usually removed for racing), and the cockpit made smaller by lowering the driving position, angling the steering column and shortening the control levers. The entire rear deck served only to carry dual spares, which were mounted above the fuel tank.*

By the time 28/95 production resumed in 1920, the engine had been updated by D.M.G. to make it more practical. The revised inline six, which had been designated M10546 in 1918, featured a new high-pressure lubrication system, operated via a gear-driven pump and a fresh oil supplementary pump, providing continuous circulation of fresh oil. In addition, a one-shot lubrication system, actuated by a foot pump, saw to the lubrication of the drive shaft, universal joint, and the steering worm gear case. Back in 1914, the cars had used foot-operated total-loss lubrication and required daily attention to 23 lubrication points and weekly servicing of 10 more!

In general, long-wheelbase versions were fitted with formal coachwork, ranging from limousines and town cars to dual-windshield phaetons, and in 1924, a sport sedan. Roadsters, sport phaetons, and a *Sport-Zweistzer* (sport two-seater) were offered on the short chassis, and on the 120.6-inch sport chassis, a rakish

*Rennsport-Zweistzer* was introduced in 1923, which closely resembled Sailer's 1921 and 1922 Targa Florio competition cars.

By the 1920s, the sporty coachwork that had appeared on models like Mercer and Stutz in America, and Mercedes, Alfa Romeo, and Hispano-Suiza in Europe, was inspiring new designs the world over, but nowhere was it considered more of a change in direction than at Rolls-Royce, which introduced the Piccadilly Roadsters, a design based upon a custom-bodied 1921 Rolls-Royce Alpine Eagle Speed Chassis bodied in Springfield, Massachusetts.

There had been sporting coachwork produced for the Rolls-Royce since the prestigious British auto maker first introduced the Silver Ghost chassis in 1907, but nothing had been as rakish in appearance as the Piccadilly Roadster, and the stunning one-off Silver Ghost Runabout that preceded it.

A runabout body design had never been attempted on a chassis as large as the Silver Ghost's 144-inch wheelbase. The result was

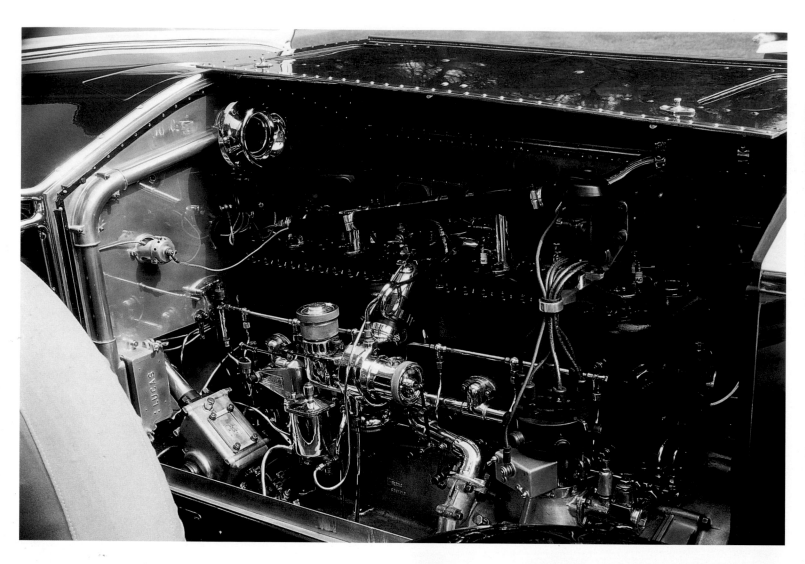

One of the most beautifully designed engines of any era was
that of the Rolls-Royce Silver Ghost. The 40-50-horsepower
straight-six displaced 7,410 cc with a bore and stroke of
114x121 millimeters. With lighter-weight coachwork like the
Runabout's, the Silver Ghost was capable of speeds in excess
of 70 miles per hour, quite substantial for a road car in 1922.

Considered to be the prototype for the Piccadilly Roadster, the
1922 Silver Ghost Runabout featured a trap seat, upholstered
in Louis Vuitton "Epi" leather.

---

surprisingly handsome, allowing for a traditional length Rolls-
Royce hood, spacious and luxuriously appointed passenger compartment, and a folding companion seat in the rear deck.

Considered the prototype for the Piccadilly Roadster, the 1921
Runabout with trap seat was built on a specially ordered chassis (No.
80LE) altered to specifications for use in the United States and
equipped with American instrumentation. The Springfield, Massachusetts, coachbuilder which produced the Runabout body for R.W.
Schutte, Esquire, the Rolls-Royce representative in New York, became
part of Rolls-Royce of America, Inc., in 1920, handling production of
the Springfield Rolls in the United States from 1919 to 1934.

The 40/50-horsepower Silver Ghost chassis were produced at
Derby in England and at Springfield, Massachusetts, in the United
States, until 1924, and remain one of the most coveted models ever
produced by Rolls-Royce.

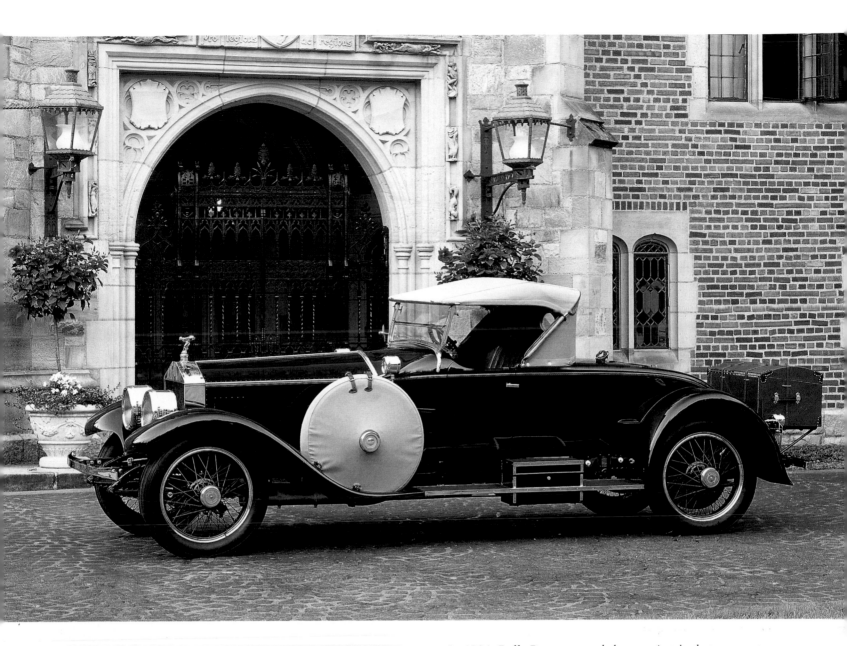

In 1921, Rolls-Royce created the sportiest body to ever grace a Silver Ghost chassis. This design, which led to the famous Piccadilly Roadsters, was bodied in Springfield, Massachusetts, and restored by owners Tom and Abby Campi. According to research done by the Campis, who are chief judges for the Rolls-Royce Owners Club (RROC), the Silver Ghost chassis number 80 LE was produced in 1920 and shipped to Custom Coachworks (later Springfield) for bodywork in 1921.

The only symbol by which Rolls-Royce motor cars have been recognized since 1910, the Spirit of Ecstacy was commissioned for Rolls-Royce by company manager Claude Goodman Johnson and created by sculptor Charles Robinson Sykes. The model for this timeless image of speed and luxury was Eleanor Thornton, personal secretary to Lord Montagu, one of the company's greatest patrons. Miss Thornton was Sykes' favorite model and had posed for him a number of times over the years for paintings, sketches, and sculptures. Her pose for Rolls-Royce has given "Thorn," as she was known to her friends, a kind of immortality.

# Chapter Three

# Birth of The American Classic— Cars from 1925 to 1941

## The Golden Years of the Automobile

What is a Classic Car? It is a term that has been so abused over the years that it now applies to almost anything built in the last century. But truth be known, nothing built after 1948 is a Classic Car. Nothing. A 1957 Thunderbird is a great-looking car, but it's not a Classic. In fact, only a handful of American cars produced between 1925 and 1948 have ever been afforded Classic status, and those that have are regarded as the greatest automobiles of their time, perhaps of any time.

The Classic Car Club of America is the governing body that determines which cars, American and foreign, meet the standards for Classic status. In short, they must be the best examples of their era, outstanding in engineering and design, and limited in production.

The quintessential American Classic is the Duesenberg Model J, a car which excelled in each of these categories. The Duesenberg straight-eight developed exceptional power for its

*With debuts in both Paris and London, the Cord L-29 was regarded by the foreign motor press as the first American automobile to capture the spirit of European design. The lower roof line (allowed by eliminating the driveshaft passing beneath the passenger compartment), bold front-end design, and flowing coachwork, as seen on this 1930 Convertible Sedan owned by Leonard Urlik, made the Cord one of the most celebrated designs of the 1930s. Wrote renowned architect Frank Lloyd Wright, who kept his L-29 for nearly 30 years, "[It] certainly looked becoming to my houses—the best design from my 'streamline' stand point ever put to market. The Cord was an innovator along right lines that changed the whole field of body design for the better."*

*The Cord engine was a Lycoming straight-eight displacing 298.6 cubic inches and delivering 125 horsepower. In 1932, displacement was increased to 322 cubic inches and horsepower to 132. The front-wheel-drive system was developed for Cord by chief engineer C.W. Van Ranst. Basically, the driveline was laid out backwards, with the differential in front, followed by the transmission, clutch, and engine. Gear change was effected via a remote linkage and a shift lever protruding through the instrument panel.*

time—265 horsepower in standard trim, and a staggering 320 horsepower with the SJ supercharger. The mechanical design by Fred Duesenberg featured dual overhead cams and four valves per cylinder, features still used in today's high-performance cars. The Model J chassis was of unrivaled strength, endowing the cars with superior handling and durability. And every one of the approximately 485 examples built between December 1, 1928, and 1937, when E.L. Cord's Auburn, Cord, Duesenberg empire collapsed, were fitted with hand-made, coachbuilt bodies of extraordinary quality and cost.

In the 1930s, a coachbuilt Model J averaged $15,000, making it the most expensive automobile sold in this country. Even Cadillac's

Harry Stutz was one of those unfortunate early automotive entrepreneurs who was good at starting companies but never able to hold on to them. When he died in 1930, he had virtually no connection with the company which bore his name. In 1925, Frederick Moskovics was brought in by new owner, Charles M. Schwab, to revamp the faltering Stutz product line. Unlike Stutz, Moskovics was as brilliant a marketing man as he was an automotive man, and he quickly dispensed with the old Bearcat styling and brought about an entirely new Stutz automobile and image. The new 92-horsepower, 287-cubic inch Vertical 8 engine and all-new body designs returned Stutz to prominence, as did a number of successes in AAA Stock Car Championship racing and a second place finish at Le Mans in 1928. The car pictured, a 1927 Blackhawk Fish Tail Speedster, owned by William B. Ruger, Sr., was one of the most famous models built during Moskovics' tenure at Stutz. He resigned in 1929.

Stutz had finally developed the best car in its history, the 1931 DV 32, an incredibly well-built automobile powered by a four-valves-per-cylinder straight-eight with hemispherical combustion chambers and twin overhead camshafts. With an output of 156 horsepower, the DV 32 chassis were fitted with some of the most stunning coachwork of the era, including models like this Weymann Monte Carlo, offered with either a steel body or the patented Weymann fabric body. As the Depression worsened, Stutz sales began to fall, and throughout the early 1930s, fewer than 1,500 cars were sold. In 1934, total sales of only six cars brought an end to Stutz production.

*Thanks to E.L. Cord's superb marketing, Auburn had earned a reputation for size and performance that made people equate them with more expensive cars. Unfortunately, this started to work against Auburn at the height of the Depression. The Auburn V-12 was more car for the money than anyone had a reasonable right to expect, and at $1,550, models like this 1933 phaeton, from the Richard Law collection, were the equal of Cadillac's V-12 convertible sedan, priced at $3,595. However, a V-12 at any price simply didn't interest buyers in the depths of a depression.*

----

great V-16 All-Weather Phaeton commanded only $7,350, and the popular V-16 Sport Phaeton, a price of just $6,500. Of course, these were also very expensive cars. To put this all into perspective, a 1932 Ford V-8 Deluxe Phaeton sold for only $545. A '32 Ford is not a Classic.

Perhaps the most-defining characteristic of the great American cars produced between 1925 and 1948 was their exclusivity. Few were made, and only the very wealthy could afford to own them. In that respect, little has changed today.

## Empire Building—
### The Saga of Auburn, Cord, & Duesenberg

Recession. There's a word no politician likes to hear in an election year, or worse, the year after. But in 1937, Franklin D. Roosevelt,

*Auburn had a long, illustrious history before E.L. Cord, but models like this 1936 852 Supercharged Cabriolet were the very best to bear the Auburn name. Redesigned for 1935 by Duesenberg stylist Gordon Buehrig and powered by a new eight-cylinder Lycoming engine equipped with a Schwitzer-Cummins supercharger, the 851 and 852 Auburns developed 115 horsepower under normal throttle and 150 horsepower when the blower was engaged by depressing the pedal fully to the floorboard.*

who had been reelected president by a landslide in 1936, was facing another economic slowdown signaled by the bears of Wall Street. The sound of belts tightening could be heard from California to New York, but nowhere was it louder than in America's automotive capitals, Michigan and Indiana.

Indiana had long been home to America's flowering automotive industry, long before Detroit in fact, but by the end of 1937, the doors would be padlocked at three of Indiana's leading auto makers—Auburn, Cord, and Duesenberg. Auburn and Duesenberg were two of the oldest names in the industry; Cord, one of its newest and most innovative, was the manufacturer of America's first front-wheel-drive automobile. The three companies were all part of Errett Lobban Cord's rapidly crumbling automotive empire, once among the most revered in the country. Auburn and Duesenberg, however, had existed long before E.L. Cord came into the picture.

Back in 1903, two Indiana carriage builders, Frank and Morris Eckhart, introduced a chain-drive, single-cylinder runabout which sold for about $800. By 1912, the Eckharts had advanced to building six-cylinder cars of exceptional quality, which they sold at very reasonable prices. Perhaps, too reasonable. Although the Auburn

was popular, the Eckharts never managed to stay in the black for long. In fact, red should have been their company color. By 1919 they were faced with a choice between certain bankruptcy or selling a controlling interest in the company to stay afloat. They opted for a partnership with a consortium of Chicago businessmen, including chewing gum king William Wrigley, Jr.

With new backers, Auburn was able to produce a line of improved models, but even with Wrigley and his monied associates holding the purse strings, the Eckharts still lacked an effective marketing organization and red ink continued to flow.

The recession following World War I cut further into automobile sales and the Indiana firm produced fewer than 4,000 cars a year from 1919 to 1922. By 1924, production had fallen to a dismal six units a day and there were more than 700 unsold touring cars sitting in the company parking lot on the day 30-year-old marketing genius Errett Lobban Cord arrived.

E.L. Cord has been variously described by historians as a "boy wonder" and a "profane, bespectacled capitalist." His claim to fame was salesmanship. Five years earlier, he had started as a salesman selling Moon cars at the Chicago agency. He quickly worked his way up to become general manager, then director of the

*The boattail speedster design that became so popular in the late 1930s was actually pioneered by Auburn in 1928 on the Model 8-115. The sporty, inverted-hull design was penned by renowned stylist Count Alexis de Sakhnoffsky and produced in three series, the 8-115 in 1928, 8-120 built in 1929, and 8-125 in 1930. Priced at a remarkably modest $1,895, this 1929 model from the Jack Dunning collection came with a 125-horsepower Lycoming straight-eight.*

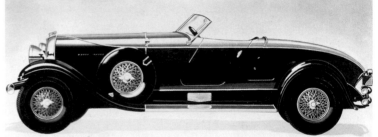

*Designed by international stylist Count Alexis de Sakhnoffsky, the Auburn Boattail Speedster, pictured here in an artist's retouched drawing of the Sakhnoffsky design, launched an era of similar speedster designs that lasted well into the 1930s.* Auburn-Cord-Duesenberg Museum

Chicago company. His reputation preceded him to Auburn, and he was immediately asked to step in as general manager.

With his finely tuned marketing skills, some paint, and a few inexpensive modifications to the foundering inventory, Cord sold the 750 leftover Auburns, which netted the company enough cash to pay off its debts. Cord was promoted to vice president and by 1926, he had ascended to the presidency and become the chief stockholder of the Auburn Automobile Company.

Under his guidance, the Indiana auto maker prospered in the late 1920s, gained a modest competition image, increased its export operations, upgraded its dealer network, and had passed an annual sales goal of 20,000 cars by the time the New York Stock Exchange plunged over the edge in October 1929.

In spite of the Depression, Auburn production soared to a record 32,301 units in 1931, the result of Cord's dealer expansion program, plus an all-eight-cylinder line of beautiful, luxurious, and bargain-priced models.

Unfortunately, the "stock market adjustment," as some auto industry pundits naively labeled it, was deepening by 1932, the year it caught up with Auburn and plunged sales to a dismaying 7,939 units. The following year they fell even lower, to 4,636, and in 1934 only 4,703 cars were sold. By then, Cord's finances were spread pretty thin.

In addition to his aviation businesses (consolidated in 1933 under American Airways—what is today American Airlines), Cord, in less than a decade, had purchased Auburn; the Lycoming engine company; Duesenberg; the Limousine Body Company of Kalamazoo, Michigan; the Connersville, Indiana, and Central Manufacturing body companies; and launched the all-new Cord L-29 front-wheel-drive automobile. He had also put himself in the enviable position of

In 1929, E.L. Cord introduced America's first production front-wheel-drive automobile, the L-29. Although Ruxton also came out with a front-wheel-drive model, Cord was first, and Ruxton was gone within a year. The innovative new design caught on with a few well-heeled East and West Coast socialites and film stars, including silver screen idol John Barrymore, who purchased this long-wheelbase Town Car built by the Walter M. Murphy Company in 1930. With all the character of a Duesenberg, the design was the work of stylist Phil Wright, who, like Murphy design chief Frank Hershey, was a GM Art & Colour Section alumnus. Murphy built two long-wheelbase L-29 Town Cars; the second was for actress Lola Montez. A short-wheelbase version was also built for petite movie star Dolores Del Rio. The John Barrymore Town Car is now part of the Jerry J. Moore collection.

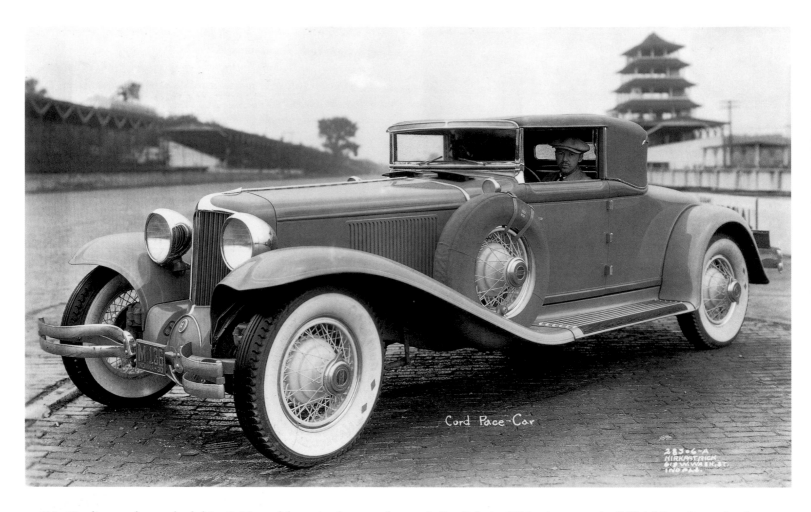

*E.L. Cord's new front-wheel-drive L-29 model was in the manufacturer's limelight in 1930, chosen as the Official Pace Setter for that year's running of the Indianapolis 500. As luck would have it, the winning race car in 1930 was a front-wheel-drive Miller, the very car upon which the Cord's engineering was based!* Author photo collection

controlling virtually every company involved in the manufacturing and supplying of components for his automobiles. By the mid-1930s, E.L. Cord had become a miniature General Motors. Unfortunately, to survive the Depression, Cord needed to *be* General Motors.

Cord's various companies offered a complete range of cars, from the lowest-priced Auburns, selling for as little as $675, to the regal Model J Duesenberg, with an average price of $15,000. What caught Cord unprepared was the length and severity of the Depression, combined with unexpected difficulties manufacturing the L-29 Cord, and delays in producing the new 1936 Cord 810.

Auburn, which should have been doing well, was suffering a loss in sales for being too much car for the money! The new V-12 models, introduced in 1932 at an average price of only $1,200, were simply not selling, even though they were priced at nearly half that of a comparable Cadillac V-12. In the depths of the Depression, few people wanted a V-12 at any price.

In an effort to save Auburn, which had spent $500,000 to redcsign the 1934 model line, Duesenberg president Harold T. Ames was put in charge of the company. He brought with him designer Gordon Miller Buehrig and engineer August Duesenberg.

Buehrig was given a modest $50,000 budget and told to do what he could to upgrade Auburn styling for 1935. "With a $50,000 budget, we couldn't do much," Gordon said later. "The decision was made to do nothing to the chassis or body and concentrate on the front end sheet metal and fenders."

Augie Duesenberg was handed the 1935 eight-cylinder engine assignment, in conjunction with Schwitzer-Cummins and Lycoming, which yielded a new 279.2-cubic inch engine developing a maximum of 150 horsepower. The redesigned cars were introduced in June of 1934 as 1935 models, and the same designs were carried over into 1936.

Despite what could only be termed a brilliant line of cars—cabriolets, broughams, phaetons, and sedans, as well as the supercharged 851 and 852 models—total production over the next two years amounted to only 7,000 cars. The 1937 models never arrived.

By sales numbers alone, Duesenberg was never a success under the proprietorship of Cord. From 1928 to 1937, only 485 cars were built, and that is believed to be a slightly exaggerated estimate since some were rebodied and others suffering mechanical difficulties fitted with replacement engines, adding to the total number of Duesenberg straight-eights delivered. But sales were not of great concern when it came to the cars of Fred and August Duesenberg. It was image. The Model J and supercharged Model SJ were the most magnificent automobiles manufactured in America, if not the world. That meant more to E.L. Cord than sales.

Back in 1903, the same year Frank and Morris Eckhart started business in Auburn, Indiana, Fred Duesenberg was beginning an apprenticeship at Thomas B. Jeffery & Co., makers of Rambler automobiles in Kenosha, Wisconsin. There he picked up a knowledge of manufacturing that would serve him well in the coming

A handsome 1930 Cord L-29 Cabriolet, owned by John McMullen, is equipped with all of the available options, including stylish Woodlite headlights. The Cord was a superbly detailed automobile inside and out with an ornate instrument panel featuring drum-type gauges behind medallion-style face plates.

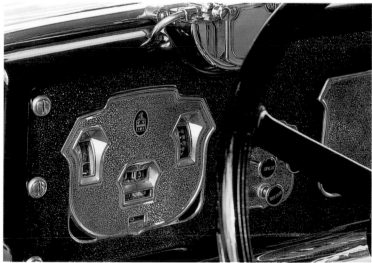

*The L-29 was replaced with the Gordon Buehrig-designed Cord 810. Produced for only two years, the innovative 810 and supercharged 1937 812 are among the most desirable of all American Classics. The 812 models are distinguished by their Duesenberg-inspired flex pipe exhausts, originally added, without E.L. Cord's knowledge, by stylist Alex Tremulis and engineer Augie Duesenberg. They drove two prototypes to New York and added them to the Cord display at the 1937 Auto Show. When Cord saw them he asked Tremulis why he hadn't been told about the cars. Alex, still in his early twenties, fired back that he "...hadn't had time and thought it would make a pleasant surprise." Cord replied, "It's God Damn lucky for you that I like it." The car was the hit of the show and E.L. gave Tremulis a $25 a month raise. This magnificent Cord is part of the Jerry J. Moore collection.*

years. In 1904, he went to work as a machinist at the first auto repair garage in Des Moines, Iowa, and two years later was running his own Des Moines garage and a sales agency for Ford, Gale, Acme, Queen, Rambler, and Marion automobiles. He was successful at this, but Fred knew that his destiny lay elsewhere. He had definite opinions as to how engines should be designed and how an automobile should perform. Fred Duesenberg wanted to build cars.

With backing from Edward R. Mason, a wealthy attorney in Des Moines, Fred was given the opportunity to pursue his passion. His first car, aptly named the Mason, was introduced in 1904.

From the beginning, Fred Duesenberg used motorsport competition to promote sales, entering a Mason in the July 4th hill-climbing contest sponsored by the Automobile Club of Des Moines. The Mason won, and Masons continued to win sporting events throughout their first year of production.

In 1907, he fitted a bare chassis with bucket seats and a lower steering post and went dirt-track racing. By 1908, Masons were winning everything from hill-climbs to reliability runs. That was the year Ed Mason decided it was time to expand. He took in a partner, Senator F.L. Maytag, who brought with him a group of

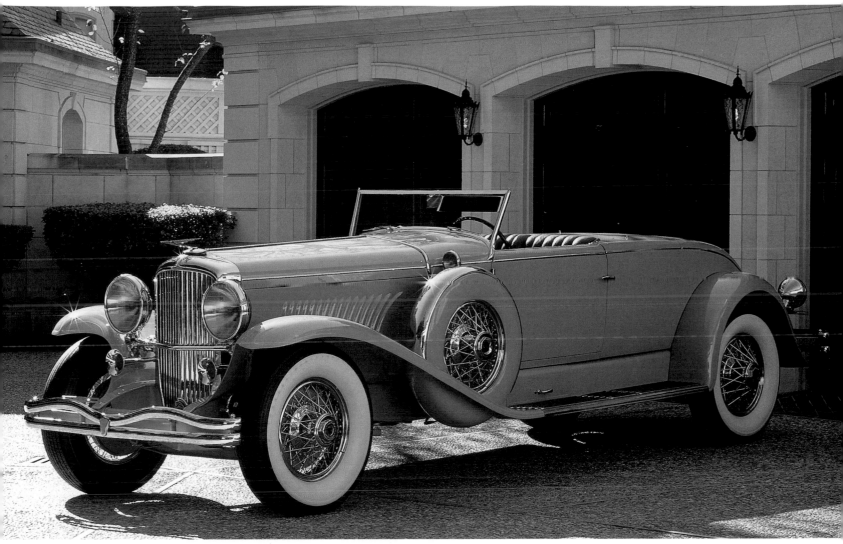

The Walter M. Murphy Company produced about 50 Model J Duesenberg Convertible Coupe bodies. Among the rarest were the long-wheelbase versions of which only two were built, J-377 and the car pictured, J-470. Both featured longer decks, slightly wider doors, and completely disappearing convertible tops.

Clark Gable and Gary Cooper were two of E.L. Cord's favorite customers. Both film stars were automotive enthusiasts, and both could afford the very best. In 1935, Gable and Cooper each ordered a supercharged Model SSJ, the only two examples ever built on an extra-short 125-inch wheelbase chassis; the car pictured was Gary Cooper's. The custom bodies were built by the Central Mfg. Co., in Connersville, Indiana; Duesenberg's proprietary coachworks.

*Duesenbergs were often bodied more than once. J-212, known today as the "Mudd Coupe" or SJ Aerodynamic Coupe, was originally a 1929 Derham-bodied Sports Sedan. In 1932, Dr. Seeley G. Mudd of San Marino, California, purchased the car and had it rebodied by Bohman & Schwartz into a progressively styled Aerodynamic Coupe with an all-fabric body. The structure of the car is framed with 1-1/2-inch ash and covered with a color-impregnated, pebble-grain Zapon cloth, resembling leather in appearance and texture. Between the outer skin and interior panels is a padding of cotton waste, tacked and stitched to the framework and backed by muslin or oil cloth for waterproofing. The supercharged engine was also fitted with a set of the rarely seen 8-port Monel metal exhaust pipes. This car is now part of the Joseph Murphy collection.*

wealthy investors. In November 1909, Mason was reorganized as the Maytag-Mason Motor Company.

In competition, Duesenberg's cars were almost unbeatable, and sales were climbing faster than a Maytag-Mason up a hillside. But for Fred Duesenberg, there were too many cooks in the kitchen, and his role in the company as superintendent and head engineer was becoming less consequential. When his design for a new four-cylinder engine was rejected because it was cheaper to purchase ready-made engines from an outside vendor, Fred left and returned to selling automobiles.

He had been right about management. In the summer of 1911, Maytag-Mason collapsed under its own weight. Maytag went into the lucrative washing machine business the following year, and Edward R. Mason reclaimed the foundering concern, reorganizing it as The Mason Motor Company. He also brought Fred Duesenberg back into the business, along with his younger brother Augie, and both were left to work on engineering developments and race cars. Their competition models were known as Duesenberg-Masons, but in racing circles, simply as Duesenbergs.

By the end of 1914, Fred and Augie had moved to St. Paul, Minnesota, and set up operations as the Duesenberg Motor Company. Their racing engines were turning up everywhere on the

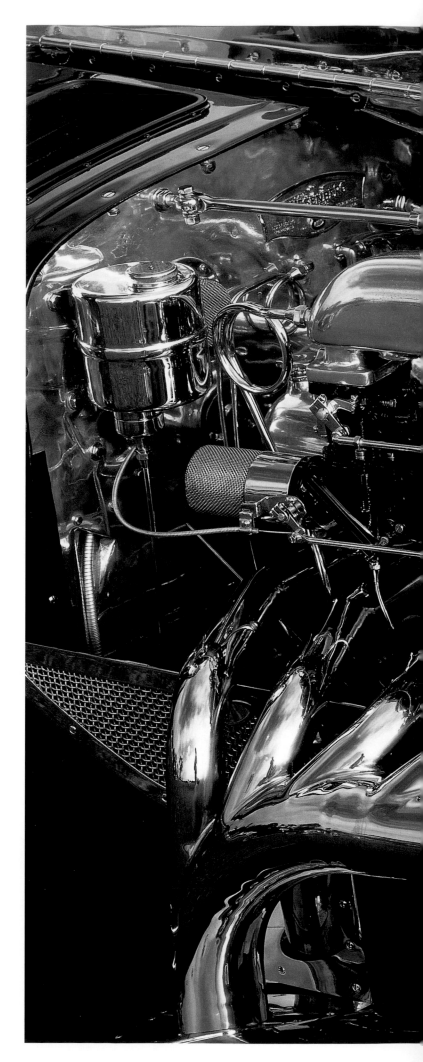

*One of the most popular of all Duesenberg designs, the Murphy Convertible Sedan was designed by Frank Hershey and produced in more numbers than any other Model J body. Production began early in 1929, and through 1930 a total of 24 were built in this specific style on the short 142-1/2-inch wheelbase; another 44 of similar style were on both the short- and long- (153-1/2-inch) wheelbase chassis. This specific car, J-208, was used as an auto show exhibit car in 1930 and 1931 and then sold. It is owned today by noted Beverly Hills car collector Bruce Meyer.*

---

*In 1931, the V-16 Sport Phaeton was selected as the "Official Car" of the 19th Indianapolis 500. This is not to be confused with the Indy 500 Pace Car that year, which was also a Cadillac, the new V-12 Roadster pictured.* Author photo collection

national motorsports scene, including the Indianapolis 500, where a Duesenberg finished second in 1916.

The Duesenberg brothers had also dabbled in the marine engine business, and when the United States entered World War I in April 1917, demand for marine engines soared, and they formed a joint venture with the Loew-Victor Engine Co. to build engines for the U.S. Navy and the Allied forces. Unfortunately for Fred and Augie, they did not control the company, and after the war the marine engine division was sold out from under them to the Willys Corporation. With new investors to back him, Fred established the Duesenberg Automobile & Motors Company of Indianapolis, Indiana, in 1920, and the first Duesenberg passenger car was introduced that year at the New York Auto Salon.

The new car offered two features that appeared for the first time in an American automobile: a straight-eight engine and four-wheel hydraulic brakes. In 1921, the Duesenberg name also became well-known in Europe when a factory race car driven by American Jimmy Murphy beat Europe's finest to win the French Grand Prix.

*One of the most popular Cadillac V-16 body styles was the Sport Phaeton, an elegant stretch of open car with dual cockpits and a retractable rear windshield mounted in the front seatback. The Sport Phaeton has become one of the most prized of all sixteen-cylinder models. With a cataloged price of $6,500, a total of 85 Model 4260 Dual Windshield Sport Phaetons were produced. This example was sold to film star Richard Arlan through Don Lee Cadillac in Los Angeles on June 6, 1930. It was later used in the 1969 film* The Carpetbaggers *and driven by star Alan Ladd, who played Nevada Smith.*

Although the Duesenberg straight-eight chassis were fitted with bodies by several of America's leading coachbuilders, the Model A Duesenberg was not a strong seller. This was not necessarily due to the cars, which had been superbly engineered by the Duesenberg brothers, but rather poor management by company executives, most of whom were replaced in 1923, the best sales year Duesenberg would post throughout Model A production.

For the most part, the company's sales and operating problems were out of Fred and Augie's hands, since the Duesenberg Automobile & Motors Company, as with previous ventures, was theirs only in name. The brothers' privately owned side venture, building race cars, was doing pretty well, however. They entered four of their Duesenberg Specials in the 1924 Indianapolis 500, claiming the checkered flag with America's first supercharged race car. Having never finished better than second, Fred Duesenberg cherished the 1924 victory at Indianapolis as his greatest racing achievement.

The reputation of Duesenberg production cars benefited greatly from the Indianapolis victory, but sales were still far from breaking records. In fact, by 1924, the company was in receivership. The fol-lowing year Fred spearheaded a reorganization, exchanging his engineering hat for the presidency of the reorganized Duesenberg Motors Company, but it was an almost hopeless situation.

For several years E.L. Cord had been watching Duesenberg from afar. An admirer of Fred and Augie's creative genius, Cord deplored the sloppy management that had driven the company to the brink of failure. In 1926, he finally stepped in, purchasing a controlling interest and reorganizing the business, this time as Duesenberg, Inc. With Cord's financing, Fred Duesenberg was again free to resume his role as an engineer, and this time he had a goal—to design for E.L. Cord the finest, fastest, and most powerful production automobile the world had ever seen. Two years later he delivered the mighty Model J, a massive, 153-inch wheelbase car capable of reaching 116 miles per hour. By 1937, it would become the most successful failure in automotive history, and along with Auburn and Cord, the most famous names on a list of once-grand American marques that never made it to the 1940s. Fred Duesenberg would never know. He died from pneumonia in 1932, at the age of 55.

*Ever wonder how people put luggage in those large detachable trunks? Some models, like this Cadillac V-16, came with a set of hard-sided, leather-trimmed suitcases designed to fit the trunk.*

## Creating the Standard of the World

Cadillac is one of America's oldest and most respected automotive names. During the 1930s, when many American auto makers offered a variety of products (for example, Ford and Chrysler manufactured cars in virtually every price range), Cadillac had only one ambition—to produce the finest luxury automobiles in the world. As the crown jewel of General Motors, Cadillac was free to pursue that goal knowing it had the financial strength of the country's largest and most powerful company behind it, and the General Motors luxury car division ventured further than any other dared.

In the fall of 1929, everything was being readied at Cadillac for the introduction of the most ostentatious automobile America had ever seen. Then came Black Friday. In one day, a record number of shares changed hands on Wall Street; the New York Stock Exchange went into free fall, and listed equities lost $26 billion in value. All in all, not a good day. The world was about to plummet into the worst economic catastrophe of the twentieth century, just as Cadillac prepared to introduce the most expensive car in its history, the V-16. Timing is everything.

It is ironic that the greatest automobiles of the classic era were designed and built during the 1930s. In the opinion of many modern day collectors, the best of the lot came in 1932 and 1933, just as the Depression hit its stride and America lost faith in the government's ability to reignite the economy. By the

end of 1932, more than 11 percent of Americans, 13.7 million people, were out of work, including President Herbert Hoover.

Two years earlier, on January 4, 1930, the effects of the stock market crash hadn't yet been realized. At the fashionable Waldorf Astoria Hotel, the annual New York Automobile Show opened and Cadillac formally introduced the all-new V-16 model. The car unveiled was an Imperial Landaulette, known as the Madam X, designed by Harley Earl and bodied by Fleetwood.

According to Cadillac historian Maurice Hendry, Earl was working on the car's design when he attended a theatrical version of the 1920s film *Madame X* at the Old Fisher Theater in Detroit. Earl was so taken with the mystique of the name that he convinced Cadillac president Lawrence P. Fisher to use it on the new V-16 model, which Cadillac did, except that marketing dropped the "e" at the end of Madame, the French spelling. An odd decision, since the company was named after Antoine de la Mothe Cadillac, the French colonial governor in North America who founded Detroit in 1701!

While V-16 body styles varied, the one constant in the model line was the mighty engine beneath every hood. In an era of fours, sixes, and straight-eights, the public was dazzled by the very notion of 16 cylinders. The largest automobile engine available in 1930, Cadillac's new powerplant was designed by Owen Nacker, a former engineer for Nordyke & Marmon who had been "recruited" by Cadillac in 1927. Marmon, by no small coincidence, introduced its

Cadillacs were very popular among the Hollywood film colony, and this handsome 1933 V-16 Fleetwood Convertible Victoria was built to order for Robert Montgomery. Each of the 126 V-16 models delivered in 1933 came with an engraved dash plaque bearing the number of the car and the name of the owner. Montgomery paid $7,500 for the custom-bodied car, which featured a Philco AM radio, a very rare item, and an integral trunk, a new idea in 1933. Only two examples of this body style were produced by Fleetwood.

Howard Marmon had been building technologically advanced automobiles since 1909, but his greatest achievement was the 1931 Marmon V-16, the only other V-16 produced in America. Despite the fact that the Marmon was a more powerful car, with a 200-horsepower engine and a top speed 10 miles per hour faster than the Cadillac V-16, and offered exclusive LeBaron coachwork designed by Walter Dorwin Teague, Jr., the company couldn't sell enough cars to stay in business. With prices ranging from $5,200 to $5,500, about $150 less than comparable V-16 Cadillac models, by January 1933 Marmon was in receivership. The car pictured is a recreation of the Alexis de Sakhnoffsky-designed Hayes Coupe built in 1932 and destroyed during World War II. It was redesigned by noted stylist and retired Art Center professor Strother MacMinn, and built by Chicago restorer Fran Roxas for Texas car collector Rich Atwell.

*This deep blue, 1936 Aero-Dynamic Coupe, owned by William B. Ruger, Jr., is one of five V-16 Aero-Dynamic Coupes known to exist. Says Ruger of his rare Cadillac, "The V-16s built from 1934 to 1937 had a kind of sensationalized styling that in many ways served as a transition from the classic era toward a more modern design. Cadillac managed to carry that off fairly well on many of its cars, but none better than the trend-setting Aero-Dynamic Coupe." Fastback styling became "in vogue" following the debut of the Cadillac and was also seen on Packard models, as well as several others.*

own V-16 model in 1931, giving America two great multi-cylinder cars from which to choose. Marmon, however, was too late, Cadillac had stolen the market.

If an engine can be considered a thing of beauty, then the Cadillac V-16 was by far the most beautiful of the 1930s, not as flashy perhaps as the Model J Duesenberg's bright apple green super-

charged straight-eight, but simply an elegant statement in basic black. The first automobile engine anywhere to bear the mark of a stylist, it was a striking combination of bright chrome, polished aluminum, black porcelain, and gleaming enamel, a mechanical and artistic tour de force that made Cadillac the absolute world leader in motoring magnificence.

Unlike contemporary engine designs of the 1930s, the Cadillac V-16 had barely a trace of unsightly wiring; everything was either carefully routed or concealed. Spark plugs were located on the

*By the late 1930s, automotive design was taking a new turn, and GM stylist Bill Mitchell, then a 24-year-old protege of GM design chief Harley Earl, had come up with an entirely new approach to luxury car styling. He abandoned the idea that a formal car had to be wide and tall. His new approach was to be a LaSalle model for 1938, but instead became the most advanced Cadillac of the prewar era, the Sixty Special. The stylish new model was a full 3 inches lower at the roof line and 3 inches longer in overall length than any Series Sixty Cadillac in 1938. This 1939 model, from the Jerry Fields collection, had a showroom price of $3,200, but by 1940, the popular Sixty Specials were selling for $4,500.*

inboard side of the engine, and their wires secreted beneath a styled cover in the cylinder valley.

The V-16 was basically two inline eights sharing a common crankshaft. The cylinder banks were placed at a very narrow 45-degree angle, and each had its own independent fuel and exhaust system. The engine used overhead valves, a design not previously seen on a Cadillac, and hydraulic valve adjustment, an industry first, which contributed to the V-16's exceptionally smooth and near-silent operation. With a 3-inch bore and 4-inch stroke, displacement was 452 cubic inches, which was mammoth for 1930.

The engine had a conservative rating of 165 horsepower (later increased to 185 horsepower), and power was delivered through a three-speed transmission. Not as fleet of foot as the eight-cylinder Duesenberg, a Cadillac could attain a top speed of 100 miles per hour with lightweight coachwork. Most, however, never surpassed 80 miles per hour on the open road.

Cadillac V-16s were fitted with some of the most exquisite coachwork of the 1930s. Fleetwood alone offered 54 body styles ranging from dashing Sport Phaetons, elegant Convertible Victorias, and formal Town Cars to the stunning 1934 Aero-Dynamic Coupe.

*The LeBaron Chryslers, looking suspiciously like the Cord L-29, used sharply pointed V-type radiator shells, broadly sweeping fenders, sloping, split windshields, and extremely long hoods. One of the most elegant designs of the classic era was the LeBaron Dual Cowl Phaeton body style for the 1931 CG chassis. Originally designed for Duesenberg by Ray Dietrich, one of the founding partners of LeBaron, the Dual Cowl Phaeton was also the body style of choice for LeBaron-bodied Packards. The Chrysler GC was designed by LeBaron co-founder Ralph Roberts and his assistant, sketch artist Roland Stickney. This gorgeous Chrysler is part of the John McMullen collection.*

The majority of Cadillac V-16s—about four out of five styles—were closed cars. However, open cars, like the Fleetwood-bodied model 4260 Dual Windshield Sport Phaeton, have become the most prized of the 16-cylinder models.

In 1933, Cadillac took a bold step forward in automobile design with another Fleetwood-bodied model, the Aero-Dynamic Coupe, which was shown as a concept car by General Motors at the Chicago Century of Progress Exposition. Built on a Series 452-C, 149-inch wheelbase chassis, the car featured a swept-back body with pontoon-type fenders and a streamlined fastback roofline—a look that not only influenced American automotive designs well into the 1940s but automotive styling the world over.

Beginning in 1934, Cadillac offered production versions of the Aero-Dynamic Coupe to fit V-8, V-12, and V-16 chassis. Fleetwood produced 20 of the ultra-streamlined five-passenger bodies through 1937, eight of which were mounted on the V-16 chassis—three in 1934, four in 1936, and one in 1937. Built on a massive 154-inch

wheelbase, the longest ever used on a Cadillac production car, the V-16 Aero-Dynamic Coupes sold for $8,100.

Despite the economic tide that had swept prosperity from every corner of America in the early 1930s, Cadillac managed to sell a remarkable number of V-16s in 1930 and 1931. Production totaled 3,251 cars. By 1933, however, sales of luxury automobiles were beginning to ebb, and as the Depression deepened, even those with the money to purchase a new Cadillac did not. Some were just being conservative, others were waiting to see if the administration of President-elect Franklin Delano Roosevelt could revive the economy. The V-16's average annual sales fell to 50 cars, and by the time Cadillac discontinued the line in 1937, approximately 4,000 had been built. This, however, was not the end of the V-16.

To everyone's surprise, GM's luxury car division stunned the automotive world a second time with the introduction of an entirely new line of cars in 1938 powered by an even-quieter flathead V-16.

The new 431-cubic inch engine used a smaller and lighter monoblock design based on Cadillac's 1936 V-8. The 431 developed the same 185-horsepower output, from a 3-inch bore and stroke, as the older V-16. Calling it a V-16, however, was almost an abstraction of the term. With the twin banks of eight splayed at 135 degrees, the side valve, L-head 16 was virtually flat; it was so recessed within the engine bay that one had to peer over the fend-

*The highest honor any American automaker can receive is to have its car chosen as the Pace Setter for the Indianapolis 500 Mile Memorial Day classic. In 1926 and again in 1933, Chryslers were selected to perform the Pace Car duties. The 1926 model was an Imperial four-passenger roadster. For 1933, it was an Imperial Custom Eight convertible roadster with a semi-custom body by LeBaron. Only nine were built with a price starting at $3,295. Author photo collection*

ers to even see the heads. Unlike its black-enameled predecessor, the most dominant features of this engine were two protruding oil bath air cleaners perched atop the downdraft carburetors. In comparison to the sculptured lines of the 1930-1937 engines, the new V-16 had all the character of a fallen cake. Of course, by 1938, automobile design had so changed that fender height and hood lines fairly well impeded the once-expansive view provided by raised hood panels.

Although Cadillac's new V-16 lacked the styling and grace of its predecessor, it propelled the model line successfully through the end of the decade and the end of an era in American automotive history.

*In 1932, Walter P. Chrysler had his experimental Custom Body Shop design and build a Speedster for his personal use. The Chrysler design followed LeBaron styling cues, such as the long, cowl-less hood designed by LeBaron boss Ralph Roberts for the 1932 CL Series. However, Walter P. chose to have the Speedster built on the shorter 135-inch CH wheelbase. The main body panels were aluminum, and the handsome, pontoon-style fenders were steel. Custom features were the large step plates, quad horns, and storage compartments in the front fenders. The exterior was a unique blend called Prescott Brown, and the custom interior was red leather throughout. Even the rubber pedals and floor mats were red. The car, now part of the Sam and Emily Mann collection, also had an AM radio, a feature seldom found in the early 1930s.*

## Building an Identity

What's in a name? Everything. Without names, societies couldn't function. The first order of business whenever a discovery is made? Name it. From dinosaur bones to the latest virus, everything in its place and a name for everything.

The name "LeMans," borrowed by General Motors from the famous French 24-hour race, was once attached to a Pontiac musclecar. Twenty years later GM used it for a sub-compact imported from Korea. The late, great American Motors Corporation had its own unique spin on the name game. Most auto makers would establish a name and then periodically change the model line. AMC kept the same cars and changed the names every few years!

Occasionally, a name acquires as great a significance as the company itself and becomes so well recognized that car and car maker are synonymous. For instance, it would be impossible to say Thunderbird and not know that it is a Ford. The same distinction applies to Imperial, a name linked with the Chrysler Corporation since 1926, the year Walter P. Chrysler introduced the new luxury model at New York City's National Automobile Show.

Chrysler built the company bearing his name atop the ruins of the bankrupt Maxwell Motor Company. After retiring from General Motors in 1919, Chrysler had a hand in restoring the debt-burdened Willys-Overland Company to solvency. In 1921, he joined Maxwell as chairman of the Reorganization and Management Committee and by 1923 had worked his magic again, doubling production and converting Maxwell's red ink into a $2.6 million

*Making its appearance in 1932 was perhaps the most classic of all Lincolns, the KB. Built on a 145-inch wheelbase, the cars were powered by a mammoth 150-horsepower V-12 with a displacement of 447.9 cubic inches. The KB was capable of 100 miles per hour, the goal of every great car in the 1930s. With a Duesenberg-inspired body style, this Murphy Sport Roadster was chosen to pace the 1932 Indianapolis 500. The Pace Setter was driven that year by Edsel Ford, pictured behind the wheel.* Author photo collection

---

profit. The following year, a new Maxwell model was introduced, and it was named the Chrysler. This may have seemed a bit pretentious on Chrysler's part, though no more so than for industry pioneers Henry Ford, Ransom E. Olds, or John and Horace Dodge.

Maxwell Motors sold nearly 80,000 cars in 1924, and of that tally, 32,000 were Chryslers. With a $4 million profit, Chrysler made a daring move. By issuing Chrysler stock to Maxwell Motor Corporation shareholders, he gained control of the company, and on June 26, 1925, reorganized Maxwell as the Chrysler Corporation.

The Imperial model line, introduced the following year, was the last word in styling, performance, and luxury. The name had first appeared in 1924 as a body style rather than a separate series. Chrysler showed two versions in 1924: the Imperial and the Crown Imperial. Distinguishing the Crown Imperial were rear roof quarters covered in leather or rubberized fabric and fitted with an oval-shaped pane behind the rear door glass. Many surviving photographs of the era reveal a rear-seat passenger beautifully framed by a cameo window.

In 1925, Chrysler production topped 100,000 cars and by year's end more than 3,800 dealers were selling Chrysler automobiles nationwide. In 1926, another production-record 162,242 automobiles rolled off the assembly lines. Spearheading the drive to wrest sales from Cadillac and Lincoln was the new Chrysler Imperial.

The Imperial line consisted of a roadster, coupe, phaeton, five- and seven-passenger sedans, plus a seven-passenger limousine. A custom-bodied landaulette and town car were also available on the Imperial's 127- and 133-inch wheelbase chassis. In 1926, Chrysler received the greatest endorsement any auto maker could hope for when a Chrysler Imperial four-passenger roadster was chosen as the Official Pace Car for the 14th Indianapolis 500.

Chrysler's stylish Imperial models sported bespoke coachwork created by the country's top designers, including Ray Dietrich and Ralph Roberts of LeBaron Carrossier in New York City. "In the early years of LeBaron history," said Roberts, "We were just designing cars and not actually building them. We were pretty much like architects back then. Our clients came to us for the designs and then went to a builder."

*In stock form, Chrysler's 384.8-cubic inch straight-eight developed 125 horsepower. Using a custom-built aluminum high-compression head and Stromberg carburetor, the engine in Walter Chrysler's Speedster produced 160 horsepower. It also had an experimental automatic choke, an almost unheard-of feature in the 1930s.*

*If you look back at the 1930s, even if it is through the cinematic eye of an old Edward G. Robinson or James Cagney film, you always see people wearing hats. Everybody from Chaplin to Churchill wore them. Hats made Henry Stetson rich, and he enjoyed good cars. His Southern California estate, aptly named Rancho El Sombrero, was home to this handsome brown 1933 KB Lincoln Coupe, custom bodied by Judkins. A Lincoln owner several times over, Stetson preferred the reliable V-12 models to other makes for their superb quality and understated styling. Stetson kept this car for 21 years! The Lincoln is now part of the Ron Klaus collection.*

It wasn't exactly a lucrative arrangement. LeBaron earned only $25 per drawing; a coachbuilt body sold for more than $1,000. Finally realizing where the money was, in 1923 LeBaron merged with the Bridgeport Body Company, forming LeBaron, Inc., and began assembling the bodies they designed.

By the mid-1920s, Walter Chrysler and Ray Dietrich had become fast friends and were routinely having lunch to discuss new automobile designs. In 1926, when the Imperial made its debut, Dietrich had left LeBaron and moved to Detroit where he set up his own independent design company with Murray Body Builders, catering to the needs of Chrysler, as well as Lincoln, Packard, Pierce-Arrow, Franklin, and Duesenberg.

Between Ray Dietrich and Ralph Roberts at LeBaron, Walter P. Chrysler had his hand on the very pulse of American automotive design, and he had the cars to prove it. Imperials were ranked among the best-engineered and best-built automobiles in America, and the equal of Cadillac, Lincoln, and Packard for status.

Despite a declining market for high-priced luxury cars, Chrysler did better than most in the early 1930s. The company divided the 1932 Imperial line into two distinct series, semi-customs known as CH, and built on a new 135-inch wheelbase, and CL, also known as Imperial Custom, built on a new chassis measuring 146 inches.

Chrysler sales for the year, which included 47 different styles and nine distinct series, amounted to 25,291 cars, more than Oldsmobile, Cadillac-LaSalle, or Packard. The distinctive long-hood CL series cars were only built to order, and for the model year a respectable 220 were delivered.

"The striking new long-hood design for Chrysler's luxurious CL Series," recalled Roberts in a 1986 interview with the author, "was a pure twist of fate. I saw the original long style hood on a trip to Paris in 1931. No one had done this in America so I decided to try it. I had one built on a Lincoln chassis to show Edsel Ford." Edsel was one of Robert's closest friends, and because of it, he was always brutally honest about LeBaron designs. "Edsel looked at it and said, 'It's awful. It's a terrible looking thing. The front end looks like a coffin.' I figured, oh well, I'll show it around later on. It just so happened, a couple of days later Walter Chrysler and the board of directors was coming over to look at some prototypes, so I had the Lincoln moved out into the parking lot so it would be away from the Chrysler people. Well, when they arrived someone saw the Lincoln and pointed it out to Walter. He took one look at it and said, 'My God, what's that?' I said it's just a design we're experimenting with. Chrysler was beaming, 'Can't we have that?

That long, long hood is really something.' I said sure you can have it, and that's how the Chrysler CL Imperial came about in 1932."

The low point of the Depression came and went in 1933 and Chrysler managed to increase sales by a small margin to 32,220 cars. A Chrysler Imperial roadster was once again selected to set the pace at the Indianapolis 500.

The classic era was beginning to wind down by the late 1930s, and the attrition rate among auto makers was increasing. Gone were many of the greatest automotive marques of the era. Chrysler, however, was well on the way to becoming one of Detroit's Big Three and closed out one of the greatest decades in American automotive history with the introduction of a totally redesigned series of cars for 1939.

The new models arrived just as Chrysler laid the failed Airflow to rest after four frustrating years of trying to sell the futuristic concept to American consumers. Although the innovative shape of the Airflow had proven too radical, many of its streamlining principles influenced the design of Chrysler's new models. As a result, the 1939 cars had a modern look with contoured headlights built into the fenders, a concealed luggage compartment, narrower running boards, and a unique two-piece grille that focused attention on the

*Chrysler styling had reached further into the future between 1935 and 1939 than it had in the previous decade, and there was little left to tie past and present together, save for the engine and the name. This 1939 Imperial Victoria Coupe, now part of the Jack Pinsker collection, closed out one of the greatest eras in Chrysler history, and with its more contemporary styling left Chrysler in an enviable position after World War II. Held up against any other new model for 1939, the Chrysler Imperials were leading-edge designs, inside and out.*

hoodline as never before. Chrysler would continue to set styling trends, revising its designs yearly through 1942, thus leaving the company with cars that would appear less dated when automobile production resumed after World War II.

Stylists such as Auburn, Cord, Duesenberg designer Gordon Buehrig, Ralph Roberts of LeBaron, and Raymond Dietrich were responsible for a seemingly disproportionate number of designs which have become American Classics. In fact, almost every marque touched by Ray Dietrich's hand has several models to its name bestowed this honor by the Classic Car Club of America.

Ray Dietrich had a way with the subtlety of a line, its implications and dynamics. No other designer in the 1930s could do so little to a car's appearance yet make so great a difference by changing one line. A slight variation in an angle, another crease added here,

a faint drop there, and miraculously a car had a distinctive look all its own. A *Custom Body By Dietrich* was more than a automobile, it was a signed piece of art.

Packard chief Alvan Macauley knew that long before he hired Dietrich as Packard's "Body Critic" in 1925.

"In Ray Dietrich," wrote historian C.A. Leslie, Jr., in *Packard—A History Of The Motor Car And The Company* "Macauley had found an amalgam of talents seldom assembled in a single individual. His background at the American Banknote Company eminently qualified him as a line sketch artist, while his four years at Mechanics Institute had further developed his ability in drafting, illustrating, air brush technique, surface development of body contours, and preparation of working drawings for detail parts and construction supervision. All this combined with twelve

*The high point of Packard styling came in 1934 when three versions of the Model 1108—a Dual Cowl Sport Phaeton, Town Car, and All Weather Cabriolet—were designed by Briggs and built by LeBaron. Of the three, the Sport Phaeton is considered to be the most beautiful Packard ever designed. Only four examples were built. The 1108 chassis measured 147 inches between the wheels and was powered by the Packard V-12, a 473-cubic inch engine developing 160 horsepower. This was the second largest engine for cubic inch displacement built in the 1930s; the largest was the Marmon V-16.*

years practical experience, a natural creative ability and a finely-honed knack for salesmanship."

In just a few short years, Ray Dietrich had completely revamped Packard styling, and helped create the new semi-custom line, cars that had a noticeably different appearance from Packard's standard fare but were manufactured in-house rather than by an independent coachbuilder. The Packard Individual Customs, however, cars designed by Dietrich and built in limited numbers, would become the hallmark of his career, and the best examples ever produced to bear the Packard name.

Among the finest representatives of Dietrich styling were the 1933 Packard 1006 customs, which, aside from having exquisite exterior styling, featured remarkably advanced interior designs for the period, notably a sweeping dashboard that wrapped around the

driving compartment, blending the ends of the instrument panel into the doors. Then there were Dietrich's rakishly angled V-frame windshields, used on models like the '33 Packard Twelve 1006 Sport Coupe, a design regarded by many as his all-time masterpiece.

By 1933, the Dietrich signature on a coachbuilt body had become a symbol of quality sought by those of means when acquiring a new Packard. Ironic in a sense, since the man whose name meant so much to Packard's wealthiest clientele hadn't been with the company since September 1930! Dietrich was long gone and

*Back in 1915, Packard introduced a revolutionary V-12 engine called the Twin Six. It was offered until 1923. In 1932, Packard dusted off the Twin Six name and introduced another twelve-cylinder engine available as an option on the Deluxe Eight. When the first Twin Six was delivered in April 1932, it boasted an output of 160-horsepower and a displacement of 445.5 cubic inches. Certified to reach 100 miles per hour, Twin Six (and later Packard Twelve) models came with a Certificate of Approval signed by two-time Indy 500 winner (1921 and 1923) Tommy Milton and Charlie Vincent, director of the Packard Proving Grounds. This 1932 Twin Six Coupe is owned by Jay Leno, who believes that the twelve-cylinder Packard was the finest luxury car of its day. "I'd put the Twin Six up against any Rolls Royce or European model of the same era," says Leno.*

working for Chrysler as head of exterior design when Packard stamped the Dietrich name on the 1006 V-windshield Sport Coupe, the only example built in 1933 from drawings Dietrich left behind when he departed for Walter P. Chrysler's side of town.

Dietrich designs used by Packard in 1933 were the foundation for the most dramatically styled models in years, the most important of which became the centerpiece of the Chicago World's Fair Century of Progress Exposition. Known as the "Car of the Dome," the bronze 1107 Dietrich Special Sport Sedan used the same rakish V-windshield design as the Sport Coupe. Additionally, a trio of 1933 Series 1006 Sport Phaetons, which were used as auto show exhibit cars in New York, Chicago, Los Angeles, and San Francisco, also featured the special Dietrich Sport Coupe windshield and instrument panel design.

Packard styling remained among the finest in the world throughout the early 1930s, and much of the credit goes to coachbuilders like Dietrich and LeBaron, whose names, when added to an automobile, assured customers that they were purchasing a limited-production, custom coachbuilt car.

American stylist Phil Wright is credited with creating one of automotive history's most controversial cars, the 1933 Pierce-Arrow Silver Arrow. A futuristic design built for display at the New York Auto Show and Chicago World's Fair, the Silver Arrow embodied what Pierce-Arrow, and its parent company Studebaker, believed to be the most modern designs of the era. Indeed, many of the ideas suggested by the Silver Arrow later became industry standards: recessed door handles, integrated headlights and fenders, concealed spares, and fastback body styling.

Had it not been for the Depression, the Silver Arrow might have been in the Cadillac display at the 1933 New York Auto Show instead of Pierce-Arrow's. The basic design originated in General Motors' Art & Colour Section, where Wright was working as a stylist until GM decided to tighten its belt in 1932.

The tough economic times turned out to be a blessing for Wright. Holding the drawings he had worked on at General Motors, he paid a visit to his friend Roy Faulkner. Back in 1929, when Faulkner was one of E.L. Cord's top executives, he had hired Wright to design a show car on the L-29 Cord chassis. Now Faulkner was vice president of sales for Pierce-Arrow, and Wright thought he might be able to sell his design to the elite New York auto maker.

When he laid Wright's drawing across his desk, Faulkner saw the future of Pierce-Arrow design, and immediately sent Wright to

*As an independent designer, Dutch Darrin had more influence on the automotive industry than anyone outside of Harley Earl. It wasn't the number of cars Darrin built that made him influential, but the people for whom they were built. Recalled Darrin's partner Rudy Stoessel, "The Hollywood Darrins were real celebrity cars. Clark Gable, Tyrone Power, Dick Powell, Errol Flynn, Chester Morris, Al Jolson, Ruby Keeler, Preston Foster, and Gene Krupa all owned Darrins." Darrin subtly changed just about every detail of the Packard One Twenty and One Eighty models he built. Roughly a dozen victorias, like the car pictured, were built through 1939 on the Packard One-Twenty chassis. Two additional cars were built on Super Eight chassis.*

*Photographed where it might well have been seen back in 1932, this handsome Packard 903 Deluxe Eight Convertible Sedan is owned today by actor/producer Robert Achor. Achor says that the stylish Packard, designed by Ray Dietrich and built by Murray, has a roll-up divider window for the rear compartment and removable B-pillars to make the Sedan into a fully open convertible. Usually Classic cars were owned by famous stars, but this one is the star. The Packard has appeared in the Disney film* Rocketeer, *in an episode of* "Quantum Leap," *and in both of the* Addams Family *movies.*

---

Studebaker's South Bend, Indiana, headquarters to develop a prototype model. Working with Studebaker's chief body designer Jimmy Hughes, Wright penned the final details of what was to become the 1933 Silver Arrow.

Today, the design and construction of a concept car could take years. In 1932, Pierce-Arrow spent a total of eight weeks from the time Wright was hired and funds for the project were allocated on November 1, 1932, until the first car was completed! Of course, to accomplish this, a crew of 30 craftsmen worked day and night on the second floor of Studebaker's engineering building. The Silver Arrows were assembled by hand, with the body panels pounded into shape over hardwood hammer forms and then welded to the body framework. On New Year's Day, 1933, the first Silver Arrow

was ready for delivery to the New York Auto Show. Thereafter, Silver Arrows were finished every 12 days until a total of five had been built. The second, fourth, and fifth cars were dispatched to Pierce-Arrow headquarters in Buffalo, New York. The third went to the Century of Progress exhibit in Chicago, where it vied for attention with Ray Dietrich's bronze Packard Twelve "Car of the Dome," Harley Earl's V-16 Cadillac Aero-Dynamic Coupe, and Gordon Buehrig's stunning Duesenberg Twenty Grand sedan. Of the five Silver Arrows built, only three exist today.

The classic era had its highs and its lows, and during the latter many of the greatest auto makers this country has ever known found themselves reaching a crossroad from which there was no return. Among them was Franklin.

The 1940 through 1942 Darrin models were manufactured in the old Auburn plant in Connersville, Indiana. Darrin production at Connersville numbered upwards of 50 victorias, a dozen convertible sedans, and three sport sedans. One of the last Packard Darrins built, this dark green One-Eighty Victoria was restored by noted Packard collector Robert Turnquist.

The Packard Dietrich 1006 customs had that rare combination of elegance and dazzling style—subtle, yet impossible to overlook. And what held true in 1933 has changed little in over 60 years. This Dietrich Sport Coupe, owned by Ronald Benach, is still one of the most dazzling closed cars ever built, accented by a rakish windshield angle and sweeping fender lines. Ray Dietrich didn't do much to make a car special, but what he did always made a difference.

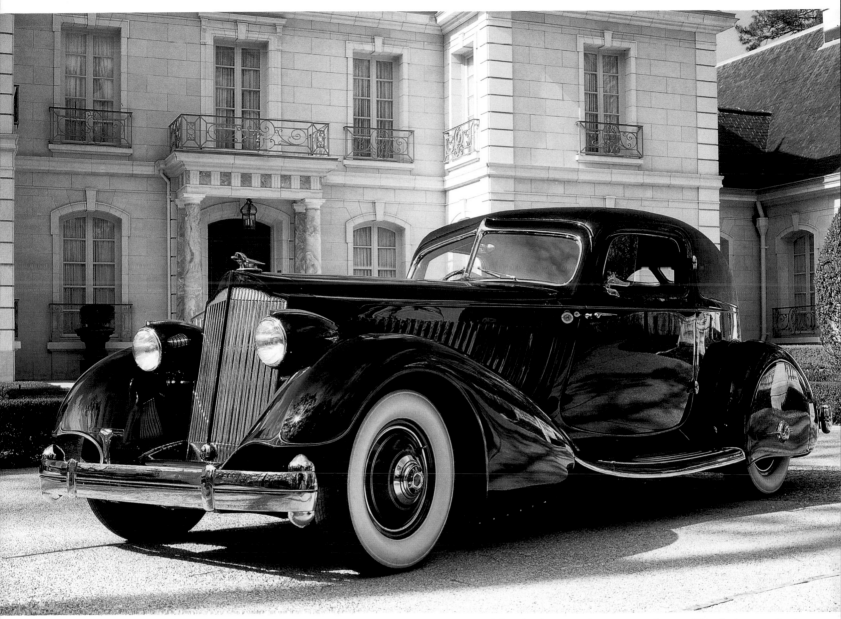

On December 6, 1933, Packard management approved construction of an 1106 model to be designated as a Sport Coupe. The sleek, fastback styling was by LeBaron. A total of four were built at a reputed cost of $18,000 each, although the selling price was only $10,000. The $8,000 loss was considered inexpensive advertising, since one of the cars toured auto expositions for over a year and another was displayed for a year at Queens Packard in New York before being sold. This car, now owned by Jerry J. Moore, was the third car built in the series and features a padded roof and blind rear quarters. Three of the original four are extant; the fourth was lost in a fire in 1961.

The Franklin was the longest-lived and most successful air-cooled automobile built in America, a car that was always ahead of its time, no matter when it was built. Franklin produced its first air-cooled motorcar in 1902, and its last in 1934.

Two of America's top aviators, Charles Lindbergh and Amelia Earhart, chose Franklins over every other car because of its innovative air-cooled, aircraft-type engine design, originally conceived in 1901 by a Cornell engineering graduate named John Wilkinson. He brought the idea to former newspaper publisher and industrialist Herbert H. Franklin, and Upstate New York venture capitalist Alexander T. Brown. Wilkinson had already completed two air-cooled prototypes for the New York Automobile Company, but the firm had neither acted on the idea nor paid him for his work. Brown convinced Franklin to take a ride in one of the prototypes, which so impressed him that he decided to form the H.H. Franklin Company and get into the automobile business.

After some litigation with the New York Automobile Company, the firm was absorbed into the new Franklin Automobile Company in 1902, and the first production version of the Wilkinson design was delivered on June 23. At the rather substantial price of $1,200 apiece, a dozen more Franklins were delivered in 1902, launching what was to become one of the most successful independent automotive marques in America.

Originally, the cars were a bit odd looking, compared to water-cooled designs, because the Franklin had no need for a radiator or grille. A robust and dependable car, Franklin built its early reputation for durability in 1904, when transcontinental driver L.L. Whitman, accompanied by Franklin representative C.S. Carris, drove a run-about from New York to San Francisco in just under 33 days, breaking the previous records held by Packard and Winton by almost a month! Although Franklins did exceptionally well in road races and endurance runs, their greatest selling point was that they never over-heated, a problem which plagued most water-cooled automobiles.

*Ed Macauley, Packard's director of design, needed someone to come up with an all-new model for 1941. He had surrounded himself with the best talent available outside of Harley Earl's Art & Colour Section at GM, and hedged his bet by commissioning John Tjaarda and Alex Tremulis to work up a proposal of their own, along with independent designers George Walker, Bill Flajole, and Dutch Darrin. It was Darrin's proposal that Macauley chose for the 1941 Packard. Macauley turned the design over to Packard chief stylist Werner Gubitz. He made some minor changes, "vandalized it," according to Darrin, by shortening the front fender sweep so that it faded out half way through the front door, raised the beltline—doing away with the stylish Darrin dip—and decreased the size of the rear window. Even with the changes, the 1941 Packard Clipper looked fantastic. Darrin had accomplished what no one had done for Packard in more than a decade—create a car that was completely new, yet distinctively Packard.*

For years Franklin prospered, either in spite of, or because of, its unusual styling. But in the summer of 1923, a contingent of Franklin dealers, led by Southern California distributor Ralph Hamlin, descended upon Franklin's Syracuse, New York, headquarters with an ultimatum: "New car, or no car." The dealers were prepared to surrender their franchises unless Franklin started building a more conventional-looking car. When H.H. Franklin bowed to the demands of his dealers, John Wilkinson tendered his resignation, and Franklin had to turn to an independent design firm to create an entirely new car. He went to the Walter M. Murphy Company in Pasadena, California, and to New York automotive stylist J. Frank de Causse, renowned as designer of the Locomobile Sportif. Franklin chose de Causse's design as the basis for the all-new 1925 model line.

Among the new cars was a long, low, and racy boattail speedster, one of the first such designs to grace an American-made chassis. With

de Causse at the corporate drafting table, a custom department was established at Franklin, and the years which followed saw an expanding line of custom bodies featuring coachwork by Brunn, Holbrook, Derham, Willoughby, Locke, and Merrimac.

Following the death of de Causse in 1928, Franklin turned to the inimitable Ray Dietrich for designs, and it was Dietrich who added the Franklin's stylish Ryan headlamps and matching parking lights.

For Franklin, the 1928 model year was to be a watershed. The Airman Series, named in honor of Charles Lindbergh, was introduced as an all-new model line. Although besieged with offers and gifts following his epic transatlantic flight in 1927, Lindbergh accepted only a new Franklin. Already an avid Franklin enthusiast, "Lucky Lindy" was also hired by the company as an engineering consultant in 1928. With Lindbergh on staff and Amelia Earhart as its spokeswoman, Franklin boasted itself as "The most comfortable mile-a-minute car ever built... the automobile's nearest approach to flying."

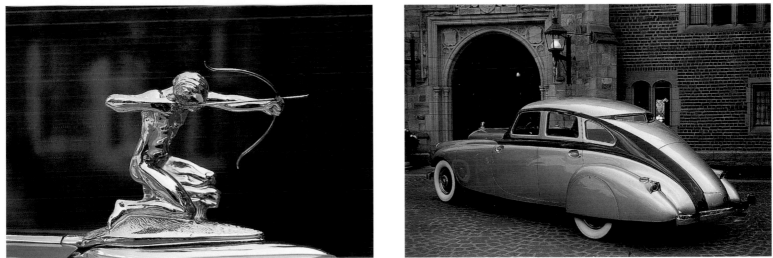

The concept was the 1933 Pierce-Arrow Silver Arrow displayed at the Chicago World's Fair. The end result was the limited-production Silver Arrows built in 1934. The green aerodynamic coupe was the first production car and the example depicted in the Pierce-Arrow sales brochure. A total of 50 1934 Silver Arrows were produced. Pictured here are the 1933 World's Fair Car, owned by the Imperial Palace collection, and a 1934 Silver Arrow, which is part of the John Labold collection.

*One of the most advanced automobiles of the 1930s was the supercharged Franklin V-12, which had the largest and most powerful air-cooled automobile engine ever built. Franklin introduced the V-12 models in 1932 to compete with Cadillac, Lincoln, and Packard twelves. This 1933 Seven-Passenger Sedan, now owned by Len Urlik, was one of four cataloged body styles, the others being a Five-Passenger Sedan, sporty Club Brougham, and luxurious Seven-Passenger Limousine. The V-12 was Franklin's best car ever, but it came too late to save the company, which closed its doors at the end of the 1934 model run.*

Franklin's biggest year ever was 1929, with production reaching 14,432 cars, but by 1932, the Depression was weighing heavily in Syracuse. Franklin sales had more than halved each year through 1933, and in 1934 Franklin would be forced to close its doors after selling only 360 cars in 1933.

The company did, however, go out with a bang. In the fall of 1932, Franklin brought out what was perhaps the best multi-cylinder automobile of the era, powered by a supercharged, air-cooled 6.8-liter V-12 delivering 150 horsepower. Fitted with sleek, LeBaron-designed coachwork, the Franklin V-12s were absolutely awe-inspiring.

By the time Franklin sold its patents to the Air-Cooled Engine Company—later called the Franklin Engine Company,

which supplied Preston Tucker with the motors for his innovative rear-engined Tucker Torpedoes in 1948—a total of 200 V-12 Franklins had been delivered. Ironically, the best car in the company's 32-year history was its last.

By February 2, 1942, when civilian automobile production came to an end and the last American car of the prewar era rolled off a Detroit assembly line, more than half of the manufacturers who had established the American automotive industry had been forced to close their doors. Gone were Auburn, Cord, and Duesenberg, Marmon, Stutz, Mercer, Pierce-Arrow, duPont, Peerless, Franklin, Kissel, and Cunningham, among others. What remained in their wake were the best examples of automotive design and engineering from the late 1920s and 1930s. The cars that would become American Classics.

*A car that history can never forget, the 1940 Lincoln Zephyr Continental launched a dynasty. Inspired by European cars of the late 1930s, Edsel Ford had the first Continental designed for his personal use. When he drove it around Boca Raton, Florida, in 1939, he received so many requests from wealthy friends that he decided to put it into production for 1940. The first 50 cars, of which this example, now in the Bob and Ginny Cressey collection, was among, were virtually hand-built in one corner of the Lincoln assembly plant using the V-12 Lincoln Zephyr as a foundation for the custom body. Originally a Zephyr model, in 1941, the Continental name was adopted and it became an individual model line. Both Cabriolets and Club Coupes were produced through 1942, and again after the war until 1948.*

*For the first postwar running of the Indianapolis 500, a 1946 Lincoln Continental was chosen. Henry Ford II, at the wheel, was the Pace Car driver that year. Front-end styling was revised from the 1942 design and even busier looking with a larger double grille. The 292-cubic inch engine was updated from 1941 with a larger positive-gear oil pump, redesigned hydraulic valve lifters, and modified crankshaft damper and fan hub. Compression was also increased to 7.2:1. Author photo collection*

# Chapter Four

# Continental Classics—European Coachwork, 1925 to 1947

*Carrosserie, Karosserie, Carrozzeria*

Every great car built during the classic era was actually comprised of two cars—the chassis and the coachwork. Each without the other was incomplete, but a great chassis and powerful engine clothed in an unattractive body was far worse than a mediocre chassis surrounded with exquisite coachwork by one of Europe's leading designers. In the 1930s, the coachbuilders held the key to success; all the manufacturers held was the key to the ignition.

## Carrosserie

Throughout the mid- to late-1930s, France became the center of automotive design, development, and manufacturing in Europe. Certainly Daimler-Benz was the undisputed leader in automotive engineering, but when it came to building exquisite-looking automobiles, all eyes turned toward France.

In the 1930s, the styling and construction techniques used by French coachbuilders were considered among the most advanced in the world, and their flamboyant, avant-garde, almost larger-than-life designs drew the stars of the

*Henri Chapron's studio at 114 rue Aristide continued to manufacture coachbuilt cars after World War II, as well as tending to the restoration of Chapron-bodied cars built for over five decades. The 66-year-old establishment closed its doors on December 30, 1985, seven years after the death of Chapron at age 92. In 1939, Chapron designed and built this Delage D.8.120 body as an addition to the French Pavilion display at the New York World's Fair. Like the other Delages, it never returned to France. It was later owned by RKO studios and used in the Gene Kelly film* An American In Paris. *It is now part of the Peter Mullin collection.*

As designed by Jean Bugatti, and built by Gangloff, the Type 57 Stelvio had skirted fenders connected by a wide running board and a high, curved trunk lid. This Type 57S example, bodied by Gangloff of Colmar in October 1937 for the Pernod family, shows a modified Stelvio body fitted with pontoon fenders and a rear deck lid design similar to that of the 1937 Type 57S Atalante Coupé. It is believed that only three Type 57S Bugatti chassis were fitted with a Stelvio body of this style. This rare Bugatti is owned by Jerry J. Moore.

In addition to being an automaker, Ettore Bugatti was also a horseman, with a fine stable of thoroughbreds. The traditional Bugatti horseshoe grille was a trademark of every model built from race cars to touring cars.

*A mixture of old traditions and new ideas, the Type 57 models abandoned the costly nickel-silver radiator shell in favor of a chromium-plated false shell with thermostatically controlled shutters. Later Type 57SC models, such as the stylish Atalante Coupé, introduced a rakish V radiator, distinguishing further this most exotic of all Type 57 Bugattis.*

*Bugatti Type 57 interiors were never overstated. Jean Bugatti leaned toward purely functional instrument panel designs with Jaeger gauges. All of the cars were right-hand drive, and had pronounced idle and spark advance controls—two long levers—positioned to the right of the steering wheel. This example is equipped with the standard floor-mounted shifter, however, a Cotal pre-selector was offered as an option.*

silver screen and the Great White Way, heads of government, industrialists, and café society from two continents. Saoutchik, Figoni et Falaschi, Hibbard & Darrin (later Fernandez and Darrin), Henri Chapron, Letourneur et Marchand, Jean-Henri Labourdette, and the Franay Brothers, all at various times, and on a variety of European and American chassis, presented some of the most magnificent automobiles ever built. World War II would bring it all to a sudden and rather chilling end by 1940.

A decade earlier, Paris was *the* center of activity with France's preeminent design studios catering almost exclusively to national marques such as Talbot-Lago, Delage, Delahaye, and Bugatti.

Among the great French auto makers, Bugatti is perhaps the most revered. Ettore Bugatti was to the small region of Alsace,

France, what Henry Ford was to Dearborn, Michigan. From around 1910 to 1951, nearly 8,000 cars bearing the Bugatti signature were produced at the factory works in Molsheim, and of the 52 different models manufactured over five decades, the most celebrated non-racing Bugatti ever built was the Type 57.

A design and engineering masterpiece, the Type 57 chassis were fitted with stunning body designs created by Ettore's son Jean. From his drafting board came the awe-inspiring Atlantic coupé; the dashing Ventoux; the luxurious, four-door, pillarless Galibier sedan; the elegant Atalante coupé; and the sporty Stelvio touring cabriolet, cars that have come to be regarded as the epitome of classic French styling.

It was in 1932, after becoming acting director, that Jean first began to influence design and engineering at Molsheim. His father

*Was it, as some have speculated, Ettore Bugatti's sensitivity to the Cubist movement of the 1920s that inspired the damascene-finished rectangular shape of Bugatti engines, or was there a more practical reason for their unique appearance? It was the latter, Roland Bugatti told noted historian Griff Borgeson. "The Boss (as Ettore was referred to) did not tolerate the waste of time, labor, or materials. Slab-sided construction was the most simple, and there you have it."*

had removed himself from the day-to-day operations and moved to a new office in Paris along the *rue Boissiere*, where he was completing work on a streamlined locomotive which would be powered by up to four Type 41 Royale eight-cylinder engines. In mid-1933, the Bugatti *autorail* set new commuter train standards in France, reaching speeds of up to 93 mile per hour. The *autorail* was Ettore's crowning achievement. The fleet of 79 sleek commuters provided excellent service for nearly 25 years.

The Type 41 Royale, on the other hand, has often been referred to as "Ettore's Folly," the largest and most luxurious automobile ever built, but with a bare chassis price estimated at $25,000 in 1930, too costly for anyone to afford. Only six Royales were ever produced and of those only three were sold. The remaining cars were in the Bugatti family until after World War II. Today they are the most valuable Classic automobiles in the world, with an average value of over $10 million each.

In 1932, Jean Bugatti embarked upon the production of the Type 57, a design somewhat more practical than many of his father's, and suitable to supporting a variety of coachwork, from sporty cabriolets and coupés to luxury sedans. The new Type 57 would not suffer the compromises of sharing its chassis design with a race car, as had earlier Bugatti models. The Type 57 would be

The stylish Ventoux four-passenger Coupé was the most produced Type 57 model. Two versions were offered: the four-light (pictured) and two-light, the latter featuring a higher roof line and no rear quarter windows. This custom-bodied example by Gangloff, now owned by Dr. Richard Riddell, was equipped with a large two-way sunroof, that could be opened over either the front or rear seats, slightly longer doors, a recessed license plate opening, and full width apron between the fenders.

This one-off design by Vanvooren was copied from a Figoni-bodied Delahaye and adapted to fit the 130-inch wheelbase Type 57C chassis in 1939. The car was reputed to have been a gift from the French government to Mohammed Riza Pahlavi, the Shah of Iran. The car was in the Shah's motorpool until 1957 when it was sold to H. Jalili, a used car dealer in Teheran, for the sum of 20,000 Rials, a five-figure amount that totaled $275 in American currency at the time. The car was fitted with a unique crank-down windshield which could be lowered into the cowl. The stylish Figoni coachwork with skirted front and rear fenders inspired similar body designs by French carrosserie well into the postwar 1940s.

*From the French point of view, the Delage was looked upon as more than an automobile, it was a work of art. This stunning Cabriolet, bodied in 1938 by DeVillars, featured unique "rivetted fins" along the fenders and down the middle of the rear deck. By 1939, Delage had been acquired by its chief rival, Delahaye. The failure of Delage as an independent automaker had come in February 1935, when Louis Delage surrendered the assets of his failed company, including rights to the name, for two million francs to Walter Watney, owner of AUTEX, the agent for Delage cars in the Paris region. He promptly entered into negotiations and, on August 22, signed an accord with Charles Weiffenbach (chairman of Delahaye from 1906 to 1954), permitting the firm to manufacture cars under the Delage name. Two years later, Watney sold all of his remaining assets to Delahaye. The Cabriolet shown here is owned by Sam and Emily Mann.*

Jean's answer to the luxurious, sporting Delahayes and Delages of the 1930s, a car capable of performance without sacrifice of comfort, luxury, or convenience, the Bugatti maxim: *Puissance, Sécurité, Confort, Précision.*

The chassis design for the Type 57 retained traditional Bugatti architecture: a solid rear axle suspended by quarter elliptic springs and Telecontrol Hartford dampers, and the front a reprise of Ettore's artistically striking solid beam axle pierced at its outer corners by semi-elliptic springs; a very complicated but impressive design.

Among its innovations, the Type 57 was the first Bugatti to integrate the gearbox—a four-speed with synchromesh in second, third, and top—with the engine. A long, floor-mounted shifter was positioned to the driver's immediate left (Bugattis were all right-hand-drive), and on later models a Cotal electro-mechanical gearbox was also available. The Cotal was a clever little mechanism that positioned a miniaturized gated gearchange, about the size of a golf ball, at the

end of a stalk mounted to the steering column. The device allowed the driver to shift with the touch of a finger, moving the miniature selector through the gears as one would a full-size stick shift. A gearbox of similar design was also developed by Major Anthony Lago and built in England by the Wilson company. A version of the Wilson Pre-Selector was used by Cord on the 1936 and 1937 810 and 812.

Progressive in many ways, the Bugatti Type 57 was antiquated in others. The chassis was rudimentary in layout, and Bugatti was one of the last European auto makers to abandon the use of cable-actuated brakes. In 1937, Bugatti finally introduced a Lockheed-designed hydraulic brake system with twin master cylinders. The ride and handling were also improved with the addition of Alliquant telescopic shock absorbers.

Despite whatever mechanical shortcomings the Type 57 and later 57C, S, and SC versions may have suffered, they were nevertheless the most desirable non-racing Bugattis ever built.

The Delahaye 135M was a true road car-cum-race car, and in competition trim, like this handsome Guilloré Cabriolet, suitable for either touring or competition. Delahaye models finished an impressive number of races during their brief five-season career, including a first in the 1934 Monte Carlo Rallye and the Coupé des Alps; third overall at Le Mans in 1935; second in the 1936 Automobile Club of France Grand Prix; and first at Le Mans in 1938.

Luxurious as they may have been, the Delahaye 135 was also one of the most efficient race and rally cars of its time. Built on shortened 116-inch wheelbase chassis, competition models like this 135M Cabriolet, bodied by Guilloré in 1937, were equipped with the 130-horsepower 3.5-liter, triple carburetor, overhead pushrod six-cylinder engine and four-speed transmission.

*Inside the T150 SS, Figoni added a large sunroof (one of the first of its kind) to provide a more open, airy feeling to the oval-shaped passenger compartment. The interior was positioned so the driver's view was over the tops of the highly crowned teardrop fenders and along the low hood line, providing exemplary forward visibility.*

*Few sports cars built during the 1930s can rival the T150 SS Talbot-Lago Special by Figoni for its sheer visual impact. The T150 SS was a far more complicated design than many realized when it was introduced in the late 1930s. As with most Figoni coachwork, the power of the body was gathered around the wheels, which were enclosed in thin, flowing, independent pods separate from the body but blended to appear as an integral part of it. The doors were another masterpiece. They consisted of large, rear-hinged ovals that opened away from the body so that entry and exit from the egg-shaped passenger compartment were made easy. This beautiful T150 SS is part of the Hull & Mullin collection.*

---

The styling studio at Molsheim was Jean Bugatti's domain, and his designs, though often controversial, were the most stirring to ever grace a Bugatti chassis. According to his brother, Roland, Jean had penned more than 110 designs by 1939 when he was fatally injured in an automobile accident, road testing a car that had recently won the *Vingt-Quatre Heures du Mans*. The young Bugatti swerved to avoid a bicyclist who had ventured too far onto the road, lost control of the car, and crashed into a row of trees. The loss of Jean, and the escalating war in Europe, brought an abrupt end to the glory days of Molsheim.

Many of the designs that came from France during the 1930s may have appeared outrageous just for the sake of attracting attention, and perhaps they were, but the innovative French designers were attempting to do more than simply turn heads along the *Champs Elysées*. The cars bodied by Franay, Saoutchik, and Figoni in the 1930s and 1940s were serious studies in aerodynamics as well.

In France, there was an aerodynamic principle known as *Goutte d'eau*, literally translated, a drop of water—nature's most perfect aerodynamic shape. It gave the obsequious fenderlines of French cars new prominence, and lent itself to bold, sweeping coachwork that is still visually stunning more than a half-century later.

Two of the most beautiful cars ever produced in France were designed by Letourneur et Marchand for display in the French Pavilion at the 1939 New York World's Fair. Both were on the Delage D8.120 chassis—one a sleek cabriolet called the Delta Sport, and the second, an Aero Coupé. Letourneur et Marchand, like the majority of French coachbuilders, used the popular Surbaissée technique pioneered by Labourdette, which positioned the body over the chassis, rather than on top of it. This allowed lower, more aerodynamic exterior styling, since the interior of the car could be lowered between the chassis rails. Both of these cars are part of the Henry Uihlein collection.

---

The masters of *Goutte d'eau* design, Joseph Figoni and his associate Ovidio Falaschi, awed and often shocked the automotive world of the 1930s with custom-built bodies as outlandish in appearance as they were popular. *Goutte d'eau* was the inspiration for nearly all of Joseph Figoni's unorthodox but beautiful body styles penned for Bugatti, Delahaye, Delage, and Talbot-Lago.

The most dramatic were the Talbot-Lago T150 SS Coupés. There were no more than a dozen of this body style produced in several variations, including at least one with skirted rear and front

*A design in vogue for the late 1930s, the Delta Sport and Aero Coupé were fitted with external flex-pipe exhausts cut boldly through the hood side panel and into the right front fender.*

*The most outlandish French body of the 1930s was undoubtedly the 1939 Rolls-Royce Phantom III Cabriolet built by Jean-Henri Labourdette for wealthy New York furrier to the stars Louis Ritter. This was the embodiment of all Labourdette designs, including the Vutotal pillarless windshield, concealed convertible top, and enclosed headlights. While some might say that Labourdette's taste was questionable, his designs were nevertheless monumental, whether they pleased the eye, or as with the aerodynamic Rolls-Royce Phantom III, offended the senses of some automakers. The British say that Labourdette committed the ultimate sin, defiling the Phantom by changing the Rolls-Royce grille and shrouding it with an aerodynamic shell of his own design. It was rumored that Rolls-Royce even tried to buy the car back so it could be destroyed!*

fenders. The teaming of Joseph Figoni with auto maker Major Anthony Lago, who brought the Talbot marque back from the brink of insolvency in 1934, was perhaps the most profound success story of the era.

Lago stepped in with his own money and purchased Automobiles Talbot and Societe Anonyme Darracq, the French subsidiary of the British Sunbeam-Talbot-Darracq, virtually rebuilding it from the ground up in five years. He did this by producing sporty road cars that could also double as race cars. While the workers at the Talbot factory in Suresnes thought this was an odd way to bring vitality back into the financially bereft company, by 1937 Talbot-Lago sports cars were in contention with Europe's best, finishing first, second, third, and fifth in the French Grand Prix. Lago's cars also won the Tourist Trophy with drivers Gianfranco Comotti and Rene Lebeque finishing one-two. Raymond Sommer gave Lago a first in both the Marseilles and Tunis Grands Prix, and by 1938 Talbot-Lago was among the three top names in French motorsports. Combined with imposing Figoni coachwork, the road cars were among the most elite European models of the late 1930s.

After World War II, Talbot-Lago continued to produce exceptional cars, some of which were powered by BMW V-8 engines. Anthony Lago retired in 1958 and sold the company to French auto maker Simca a year later. Simca became Chrysler France SA, in 1970, and was sold to Peugeot-Citroën in 1979.

In 1939, there were no Ferraris or Lamborghinis to talk about. Enzo Ferrari had just resigned from his position with Alfa Romeo, where he had worked since 1919, first as a test driver and later as manager of Alfa's racing department. Ferrucio Lamborghini, still working on his family's farm in Ferrara, north of Bologna, wouldn't cross Ferrari's path for another 25 years. In the 1930s, exotic cars bore names like Lancia, Isotta-Fraschini, Hispano-Suiza, and Delahaye, names well known to wealthy American sportsmen, but of little note to John Q. Public, who at best might have heard of Jaguar, Mercedes-Benz, and Rolls-Royce. The one French name most Americans did recognize, however, was Delage. The credit for this goes to a stunning trio of cars sent over by the French government for display at the 1939 New York World's Fair.

Of the three Delage cars commissioned by the French government, the first two were built in 1938 by the renowned firm of Letourneur et Marchand and displayed in the French Pavilion

*The majority of body designs for Hispano-Suiza models were conservative, mostly traditional phaetons, cabriolets, sedans, and town cars. It was a rare car that featured the sweeping lines of this Saoutchik-bodied 1935 K6 Cabriolet, which is poignantly accented by the sculptured chrome speed lines leading back from the edge of the grille to the rise of the rear fenders, and the chromed teardrop emphasizing the fender shirt. This car is now part of the Peter Mullin collection.*

---

throughout 1939. The third Delage, designed and built by Henri Chapron, Delahaye's premier coachbuilder, was added in 1940, after the fair was extended an additional year by New York Mayor Fiorello LaGuardia. World War II prevented the cars from returning to France, and all three were sold to Americans for an estimated price of $7,500 each. They have remained in this country ever since.

While the World's Fair cars were custom-bodied examples, their styling was indicative of the advances being made in coachwork design by France's leading stylists. The sleek Delage Aero Coupé featured a *Vutotal* pillarless window pioneered by Jean-Henri Labourdette. As applied by Letourneur et Marchand, the side windows swept downward following the curve of the body and roofline but had no B-pillar or other visible means of support.

The Chapron Cabriolet was a traditionally elegant design featuring bold pontoon fenders, large, rear-hinged doors, and luxurious seating for four. A downswept rear deck, nestled deep between the fenders, incorporated a small trunk and a fashionable enclosed continental-style spare that characterized the avant-garde styling of

Chapron coachwork for Delage and Delahaye.

Of all the great marques bearing Chapron's signature, the cars that made him most famous were those designed for Delage and Delahaye. Their relationship, which began in the 1920s, lasted well into the postwar 1940s, by which time both Delage and Delahaye were added to the list of auto makers which did not survive long after the end of World War II.

Throughout the 1930s, French coachwork was on the cutting edge of automotive styling. Figoni and his contemporaries, Saoutchik, Labourdette, and Chapron, were working at a level that still bewilders auto enthusiasts better than half a century later. One can only accept that their interpretations of the automobile body were as much an art form as they were a practical means of surrounding the steelwork structures beneath.

No matter which atelier executed the body design, they created rolling works of art that have withstood the test of time, immortalizing automobiles that have not been built in over 50 years.

*This 1935 Special Roadster, also referred to as a Sport Roadster, was built on the 500K chassis. This is believed to be the sixth 500K Special Roadster bodied at Sindelfingen, and is differentiated from any other by its lack of chrome fender trim and trim around the doors and decklid, as requested by the original owner, Prince Nickolaus Leopold. This rare car is now in the William Chorkey collection.*

## Karosserie

For Daimler and Benz, the 1930s marked the first full decade of their amalgamation as a single company, an era highlighted by far-reaching advancements in engine, chassis, and suspension design that would put Mercedes-Benz at the forefront of the European automotive industry by 1940. However, what truly set Mercedes-Benz models apart from other cars of the era was the magnificent coachwork designed at the factory's renowned Sindelfingen Werk.

The city where Daimler first established a factory for aero engines and aircraft, Sindelfingen later became the karosserie for the Daimler-Benz chassis. In 1932, under managing director Hermann Ahrens, the styling and construction of custom bodies became the primary function of the Sindelfingen Werk.

Although the factory was responsible for 380, 500K, and 540K designs from 1935 on, quite a few were bodied by independent coachbuilders such as Erdmann & Rossi, which designed and built half a dozen custom versions, including the ultramodern 1936 500K Stromlinien-Limousine. Erdmann & Rossi also turned out a stunning 540K Roadster-Cabriolet in 1938 with eye-catching cut-out rear fender skirts and sweeping bodylines that looked more French

than German. In 1937, karosserie Voll & Ruhrbeck designed a Sport Cabriolet on the 540K chassis that was equally avant-garde.

The engineering of the 500K and 540K chassis with its four-wheel independent suspension, pioneered by Daimler-Benz in the early 1930s, was a remarkable platform upon which to build a custom body. Despite its tremendous weight, a 540K could accelerate from a stand to 62 miles per hour (100 kilometers per hour) in under 16 seconds and attain a maximum speed of 100 miles per hour. In 1937, any automobile that could achieve triple-digit speed was immediately legendary.

While the 500K and 540K may get all the glory today, the short-lived 1933 Type 380 introduced virtually all of the features for which its successors are revered. Total production amounted to 60 examples, ranging in style from open Tourers to Sport-Roadsters, Sedans, Roadster-Coupes, and Cabriolets A and B. Considered somewhat underpowered for its size and weight, the 3.8-liter engine was bored and stroked to 86x108 millimeters, increasing displacement to 5.0 liters (5,019 cubic centimeters) and output from 120 horsepower with supercharger to 160 horsepower. (The standard wheelbase was also increased by 150 millimeters to 3,290

*Another very rare Mercedes-Benz model, a 540K with a 500K Cabriolet A body. This 1935 example was one of the true transitional cars, ordered as a 500K on June 25, 1935, but fitted with one of the first 5.4-liter engines. It was delivered on July 15, 1935, to the Vogel Publishing House in Poessneck-Thueringenin. Kommission number 206355, with engine number 123776, it is one of 13 documented 500Ks equipped with the new Daimler-Benz 5.4-liter straight-eight. Of those fitted with the 540K engine, only three, including the car pictured, are currently known to exist. This one is in the collection of Frank Cherry.*

---

millimeters/129.5 inches.) Thus was created the 1934 500K. The final evolution of the design was the 540K, officially introduced in 1936 with an increased displacement of 5.4 liters (5,401 cubic centimeters) and a breathtaking 180 supercharged horsepower. The 540K was advertised as the fastest standard production automobile in the world with a maximum speed of well over 100 miles per hour and the ability to cruise the new German Autobahn effortlessly at 85 miles per hour.

(Note that both the 500K and 540K were additionally offered in *kurz* or short wheelbases of 2,980 millimeters for the Sport-Roadster and Sport-Coupe bodywork on the 500K and Sport-Roadster and Sport-Cabriolet A on the 540K.)

With an appearance that one journalist in the 1930s described as having "aggressive styling and Teutonic arrogance," all Mercedes-Benz 500K and 540K body designs were indeed awe-inspiring. It was that perceived image that may well have been the reason Mr. William A. M. Burden, the great, great grandson of Cornelius Vanderbilt, requested that the Sindelfingen factory build this 540K Cabriolet C to his personal specifications in 1936.

While most 540Ks had long sloping fenders, fender-mounted spare tires, and running boards, Burden's design called for more stylish pontoon fenders without running boards and a rear-mounted spare with provision for a second. It also had a unique slanted grille shell over the radiator and no exposed cap or mascot. The goal was to emulate the racing Mercedes of the period. However, the end result ended up with a distinctively French accent, resembling late-model Delage and Delahaye designs by Chapron, Saoutchik, and Letourneur et Marchand. This 540K is now in the H. Roy Jaffe collection.

*The factory photo of the William A. M. Burden 540K Cabriolet C before it was delivered. Note the car's minimal chrome trim and black wire wheels. H. Roy Jaffe*

The 540K marked a turning point in Sindelfingen design, which became noticeably more streamlined in 1936, as evidenced by the styling of the 540K Special Roadster, Special Coupe, and Cabriolet A. These automobiles are regarded today as much for their styling as their superior engineering.

Mercedes-Benz was not alone in the German luxury car field. In fact, Daimler-Benz AG had plenty of company. Among the most zealous competitors were Horch and Maybach, the latter formed shortly after World War I by Gottlieb Daimler's old partner, Wilhelm Maybach.

After leaving Daimler in 1907, Maybach joined Graf Zeppelin where he was responsible for overseeing the construction of engines for the giant airships. In the early years following World War I, Germany was forbidden to manufacture aero engines as a provision of the Versailles Treaty, so Maybach began building auto-mobile and commercial vehicle engines under the name Maybach Motoren-Werken. In 1921, the company launched its own line of luxury cars. Adding a V-12 model in 1929, the year in which Wilhelm died, Maybach became one of Germany's leading manufacturers of high-status luxury cars. Always of very conservative design, Maybachs appealed to the very wealthy who found Sindelfingen's styling for the Mercedes-Benz too flamboyant and Horch too middle class. World War II brought automobile production to an end, and Maybach built 12-cylinder diesel engines for tanks and half-track vehicles.

After 1945, Maybach continued manufacturing diesel engines. Today, the company is part of Daimler-Benz AG, and since 1960 has produced Mercedes-Benz heavy diesel engines at Friedrichshafen, under the name Motoren-Turbinen-Union (MTU).

After a three-year apprenticeship under Carl Benz, August Horch founded a company bearing his name in 1899. When Horch left Benz und Cie., he had risen to the position of plant manager for motorcar construction. Horch was an engineer of the first order, but historically, an individual who was not known for his congeniality or ability to work with others.

*Is this the most beautiful 540K ever built? Some will say yes. Of the 406 model 540Ks produced from 1936 to 1940, more than 350 had coachwork designed at the factory's Sindelfingen Werk in a variety of 11 basic styles. However, only four 540Ks were bodied as Special Coupes, the most graceful closed car of the entire classic era, and perhaps the finest design ever to come from the renowned Sindelfingen Werk.*

Horch resigned from his own company over financial disputes with investors in 1909. He then started another concern but found he had lost the rights to his name. The son of one of his new partners suggested that the company should use a Latin translation of the German word *horch* (imperative of the verb "to listen"), which happened to be *audi*. The new company was formally christened Audi Automobilewerke, m.g.H.

The original Horchwerke soldiered on without its namesake, ultimately becoming the luxury division of the German Auto Union formed in June 1932 through the merger of Audi, DKW, Wanderer, and Horch. To depict the solidarity of the Auto Union, an emblem comprised of four intertwined rings was chosen, the very same symbol used today on Audi models.

August Horch resigned from Audi in 1920 and, having run out of ways to spell his name, went to work at the Ministry of Economics in Berlin. To his former associate's chagrin, he was reinstated as head of Horchwerke in 1933 under the new Auto Union. He later became a member of the Auto Union board of directors, giving him dominion over both Horch and Audi.

The majority of cars produced in the 1930s were powered by straight-eight, single-overhead-cam engines produced in various sizes from 3.0 to 4.9 liters through 1935. Horch also tried its hand at producing a V-12 in 1929, but the engine was discontinued in

1932. Although considered comparable to the Mercedes-Benz 540K as a high-status German car, Horchs were neither as powerful nor as manageable on the road. In general, they were also priced considerably lower.

One of many German auto makers unable to rebuild after the war, because their factories ended up in the eastern sector and under Soviet control, the Horch line was not revived. By 1949 the Auto Union was able to resurrect itself in Ingolstadt, West Germany, with Audi and DKW, and in October 1964, ownership was transferred to Volkswagenwerk AG in Wolfsburg. Today, Audi is the sole surviving member of the once-great German Auto Union.

### Carrozzeria

We are living under an illusion, an illusion woven by automotive copywriters and advertising executives who use the word *new* as freely as a casual greeting. "Hi! This is new..." We have been told that innovations such as dual overhead cams, four valves per cylinder, and unitbody construction are recent developments—recent in this context being anything developed since the end of World War II. For many auto makers, these features *are* new, but their technology is old, almost as old as the automobile itself, and much of it originated in one of the least expected corners of the world: Italy.

Among the most successful of Italian auto makers was Lancia. It has been written that Lancia never made a bad car, and while that may sound like a wild exaggeration, it is hard to name a model that was not successful. Despite the fact that Lancia never achieved a lasting foothold in this country, throughout Europe the cars are as highly respected as those of Alfa Romeo.

*Not every great Mercedes-Benz of the classic era was a 540K, nor was it bodied by Sindelfingen. This very formal 460 Nürburg Convertible Sedan was bodied by Karosserie Papler in 1929. The 460 Nürburg, 460 indicating the 4,622-cubic centimeter displacement of the engine and Nürburg after the endurance race won by a 460 in 1928, was the first eight-cylinder Mercedes-Benz model. The engine was designed by Dr. Ferdinand Porsche. Although 3,800 Nürburg chassis were built from 1928 to 1939, very few of the cars remain today, and custom-bodied examples, like this Papler Convertible Sedan owned by Mark Bedsole, are as rare as any classic era Mercedes-Benz.*

*Although the majority of Maybach bodies were conservative, there were a few that had very contemporary styling, such as this 1931 8-liter Sport Cabriolet, winner of 1st Prize (Silver Flag) at the Budapest Auto Show, Easter, 1931.* Automobile Quarterly

The company was founded by Vincenzo Lancia, who started a successful racing career with Fiat in the early 1900s. A talented engineer as well, Lancia was encouraged to go out on his own by Count Carlo Biscaretti di Ruffia, one of Fiat's founders, who helped him with the purchase of a small factory in 1906. Within a year, Lancia & Cie, Fabrica Automobili had completed its first prototype automobile. Unfortunately, a fire destroyed the car in February 1907, before Lancia even had a chance to run it. Undaunted, seven months later he completed another. It was a conventional design with a 2,543-cubic centimeter (-cc), 28-horsepower, bi-bloc four-cylinder engine, four-

*In 1929, the year in which Wilhelm Maybach died, a Maybach-powered Zeppelin airship flew around the world, and the company introduced its first V-12 models, powered by a 6,962-cubic centimeter engine developing 150 horsepower. In 1930, the luxurious Maybach twelve was renamed the Maybach Zeppelin in honor of the historic 1929 trans global flight. Always of very conservative design, this 1930 two-position Convertible Sedan was indicative of the refined Maybach styling.* Automobile Quarterly

speed gearbox, and shaft drive. The model, later referred to as the Alfa, went into production in early 1908. After a run of 108 cars, it was replaced by the slightly larger monobloc 3,120-cc Lancia Beta. There was also a 3,815-cc six-cylinder Dialfa, of which Lancia produced only 23 examples. The Beta was developed into the 3,460-cc Gamma in 1910 and the 4,080-cc Delta in 1911.

With a steady demand for new models, Lancia acquired a larger production facility in 1911 at Via Monginevro on the outskirts of Turin. The 107,000-square foot factory would remain the company's headquarters throughout the late 1930s.

An innovative engine builder, Lancia, in 1919, developed a prototype V-12 that laid the groundwork for a long line of narrow V-form Lancia engines, beginning with the Trikappa V-8 in 1922. However, the design of V configuration engines wasn't new even in 1919. Gottlieb Daimler had built a V-2 back in 1888, and the advancement of the design proceeded so rapidly that by 1910 there were more than 40 different V-type engines, including the world's first design for a V-6, developed around 1905 by American Howard Marmon. However, it would take another 45 years before a production V-6 would appear, and that engine would be a Lancia design.

The company's accomplishments were not limited to engines alone. As far back as 1913, Lancia & Cie had pioneered the use of

Audi *magazine, the official publication of Auto Union's current bearer of the rings, states that the pictured Horch 710 Spezial Roadster features a chassis with a straight eight-cylinder engine built in 1934. Custom coachbuilders Reinbolt & Christe AG Carrossiers of Basel, Switzerland, built the body between 1934 and 1935. Fashioned entirely of 16-gauge aluminum, the 710 Roadster sports leather interior and rare Marchal spotlamps. It is believed that the Spezial Roadster was originally finished with unpainted polished aluminum fenders to match the polished aluminum trim around the passenger compartment and along the length of the hood. Today, the fenders are painted to match the body, a far less stunning contrast. This is the only Spezial Roadster built on the 710 chassis. Exact records of the car's delivery were lost during World War II when the Horch factory in Zwickau-Sachsen was destroyed, as were the buildings of the Auto Union general management in Chemnitz-Sachsen.*

electric starters and electric lights in Europe, introducing the first European car with a standardized electrical system. Unitbody construction—the touchstone of contemporary automotive manufacturing adopted by auto makers the world over in the late 1940s—was developed by Lancia two decades earlier with the 1922 Lambda, the world's first unit-chassis automobile. Powered by a single-overhead-cam V-4 engine, the Lambda also introduced Lancia's vertical-coil independent front suspension, unitbody construction (comprised of the chassis and lower half of the body), and four-wheel brakes. It was acclaimed one of the most important new designs of the decade.

Lancia's advanced designs and notoriety throughout Italy attracted the attention of an American businessman by the name of Flocker. According to the diary of Battista Falchetto, who was an associate of Sig. Lancia, Flocker was so impressed with Lancia's cars that he proposed setting up a Lancia factory in the United States. Having secured backing from several investors, in 1927, Flocker incorporated Lancia Motors of America, capitalized for $1 million. With great fanfare, Vincenzo Lancia and 10 custom-bodied prototype models arrived in New York City for the Importers Car Show at Commodore Hall. It turned out to be a fiasco. Flocker and several of his "partners," who proved to be of questionable character—"gangsters"—as Falchetto wrote, had established the company for the sole purpose of luring investors into a stock promotion scheme. A discouraged and angered Vincenzo Lancia departed for home and proceeded to battle Flocker for the return of the prototypes, which eventually found their way back to Italy.

*A more conventional Horch body is this 1932 twelve-cylinder Cabriolet. When Maybach introduced its twelve-cylinder model in 1929, Horch followed suit to remain competitive in the luxury car market. The Horch twelve came in two series: the 600 with a 147.6-inch wheelbase, and 670 with a shorter 135.8-inch wheelbase. Horch stylists borrowed freely from American cars like the Chrysler Imperial, to which this Cabriolet bears strong resemblance. The Horch twelve was discontinued in 1932 after two-and-a-half years of lackluster sales.*

*The Lancia Dilambda chassis was originally a long-wheelbase design measuring 137 inches. A short 129-1/2-inch chassis was added to the model line by 1930. The underslung Dilambda platform allowed coachbuilders to produce luxurious four-door sedans with low, graceful roof lines and cabriolets and convertible sedans with sportier coachwork than Lancia's British and German contemporaries. The Dilambda had a stance that could only be compared with the American-built Stutz DV 32 Weymann Monte Carlo sedan and the famous Cord L-29. This Viotti-bodied 1932 Dilambda Torpedo, owned by Noel Thompson, is one of the finest examples of a classic-era Lancia.*

While Lancia of America was a failure, the new car Lancia had designed for Flocker, based on the 1926 Tipo 220 prototype, was a critical success and the inspiration for one of the company's most celebrated models, the Dilambda, which made its debut at the 1929 Paris Motor Show.

Intended as a luxury car, the Dilambda was built on a separate chassis, sidestepping Lancia's pioneering unitbody construction, so that coachwork could be tailored by the world's leading design houses. The Dilambda carried some of the earliest work by Pinin Farina, Castagna, and carrozzeria Viotti in Italy. In England, Weymann, James Young, and Gurney Nutting bodied the Dilambda; Kellner, De Viscaya, and Labourdette in France; and the Walter M. Murphy Company in America.

Its low chassis height and center of gravity endowed the Dilambda with exceptional handling, assisted by the use of a pillar-type independent front suspension and underslung rear springs. The cars were so low to the ground that one owner described the Dilambda as "...like driving a dachshund." With a ground clearance of 8 inches, the Dilambda was bellied to the earth. "It is the safest chassis in the world on fair or foul going..." stated an advertisement by Lancia (England) Limited. In the August 5, 1930, issue of *The Motor*, the editors wrote: "The Lancia Dilambda is a car with two characters. To the sedate or elderly it is a very gentlemanly carriage: silent, refined, flexible. To the young blood, straight from the Varsity, it is a high-spirited, highly-strung, beautiful thing of nerves and sinews, a thoroughbred if ever there was one."

A total of 1,685 Dilambdas were produced between 1929 and 1935, including 20 with left-hand drive, the majority of which were sold in the United States.

Following Vincenzo Lancia's death in February 1937, management was briefly taken over by Manlio Gracco, and soon after, by Vincenzo's son, Gianni Lancia, who remained at the head of the firm until 1955.

Lancias are about as well known in mainstream America today as Kaiser Manhattans are in Turin, Italy. In fact, the Kaiser may have a slight edge. Mind you, Lancia bears no blame for this; their cars have always been among the finest built and most technologically advanced to come from Italy. Even today, Lancias, which have been manufactured by Fiat since 1969, are still very popular throughout Europe. Unfortunately, not every foreign car that was imported into this country met with the success of Mercedes-Benz or Rolls-Royce. In later years, there were numerous attempts to sell Lancias in the United States, and when Fiat had its own American distribution network, Lancias were imported and sold through select dealerships across the country. However, like Fiat, Lancia never established a strong enough foothold to remain successful. We can add to that illustrious list MG, Rover, Triumph, Jensen-Healey, Citroën, Renault, Peugeot, and Alfa Romeo. All of which have withdrawn from the U.S. market over the last 25 years.

Alfa Romeo, one of Italy's oldest auto makers, was formed in 1910 out of the failed Italiana Automobili Darracq, a division of French auto maker Darracq & Co., which began building cars in Naples in 1906. The Darracq proved totally unsuitable for Italian roads, and in 1906, after sales plummeted to only 61 cars and lost Alexandre Darracq 150,000 lire, he surrendered the Italian branch to a group of local businessmen. With a loan of 500,000 lire from the Banca Agricola di Milano, Anonima Lombardo Fabbrica Automobili was formed on January 1, 1910. Following World War I, the company was merged with Nicola Romeo & Co. to become Alfa Romeo.

Alfa made its racing debut in the 1919 Targa Florio, and from then on its reputation was maintained by the finest sports and competition cars of Italian manufacture. Alfas were held in high esteem throughout Europe and Great Britain, having scored victories in virtually every major racing event from Le Mans (four consecutive years, 1931-1934), to the Targa Florio (six straight times, 1930-1935), and the Mille Miglia (every year from 1928 to 1938!).

Until the postwar era, Alfa Romeos were essentially hand-built automobiles produced in very limited numbers. From 1910 to 1950, only 12,200 cars were built, an average of less than one car per day! Alfa Romeo's survival during the lean years of the Depression was ensured by the Italian government, which purchased sufficient shares to keep the company solvent. In Italy, auto racing was

*The Lancia Dilambda was powered by an innovative 24-degree V-8 designed with staggered bores, vertical valves, and wedge-shaped combustion chambers, making it only slightly larger in overall dimensions than the Lambda V-4. The ohv V-8 with a 79-millimeter bore and 100-millimeter stroke displaced 3,960 cubic centimeters and delivered 100 brake horsepower through a four-speed transmission. The engine drew fuel through a Zenith twin-choke carburetor and exhaled via an exhaust system that even today is considered a masterpiece of tubular confusion. Each exhaust valve had a separate port, and the four-branch manifolds on each side ran forward to be joined by pipes running down in front of the engine before making a reverse turn and heading aft!*

the national obsession, and Alfa Romeo the national champion.

Throughout the late 1920s and well into the 1930s, Alfa Romeo produced an endless stream of remarkable cars, such as the 6C 1500, 6C 1750, and the Le Mans champion 8C 2300, suitable to both road and track. Among the most popular road cars was the innovative 6C 2300B, heralded as one of the first production cars in Europe to offer a four-wheel independent suspension. The advanced front-wheel geometry of the 6C 2300B included wheels carried on paired trailing arms and controlled by coil springs and hydraulic shock absorbers. The front suspension was copied by Dr. Ferdinand Porsche and incorporated into many of his later designs. However, according to Alfa Romeo historian Luigi Fusi, this "sharing of ideas" was accompanied by Alfa's use of a Porsche-designed swing axle rear suspension in the 6C 2300B and all other Alfa Romeos produced from 1936 to 1950.

In 1939 the 6C 2300B was replaced by the 6C 2500, one of the last models built before World War II, as well as the first to be offered when Alfa Romeo resumed production in 1946.

If Alfa Romeo was the greatest Italian sports car in the 1930s, then the Isotta-Fraschini was its luxury counterpart. Were beauty alone the only reason for the Isotta-Fraschini's existence, it would have been reason enough. One would have to search long and hard to uncover an ungainly example of this proud marque, the true thoroughbred of Italian motorcars in its day.

It was in the dawning years of the automobile, before the turn of the century, that Cesare Isotta and the brothers Fraschini (Oreste, Vincenzo, and Antonio) formed a company to import Renaults into Italy. By 1902, they were producing their own automobiles using de Dion engines and Renault transmissions.

Alfa Romeo built its fortunes on small, lightweight sports models like this 1928 6C 1500 Sport Spider with coachwork by carrozzeria Zagato. The first sports car for sale to the public to offer an overhead camshaft engine with a hemispherical combustion chamber, the light, nimble 6C 1500 was designed from scratch as a sports car, the first of a line that would make Alfa Romeo one of the most recognized names in the automotive world by the end of the 1930s.

Societa Anomina Fabbrica di Automobili Isotta Fraschini, often referred to as IF, started producing its own engines in 1903 when Giuseppe Steffanini joined the firm as an engineering consultant. Their first all-Italian-built model, the Tipo 12 horsepower, launched three decades of Isotta-Fraschini engines and automobiles.

In the early 1900s, Isotta's marketing and sales priorities were directed not wholly toward Europe, as one would have expected, but far across the Atlantic to the eastern seaboard where race-prepared Isottas won the 1908 Briarcliff in New York, the Lowell Trophy in Massachusetts, and the Savannah Challenge Trophy race in Georgia. The strong showing by the Milanese firm resulted in the marque's rapid climb in popularity among America's automotive elite.

Giuseppe Steffanini's work for IF—his last recorded design executed in 1914—was overshadowed by Giustino Cattaneo, who

joined Isotta in 1905 as technical director. For the next 30 years, virtually all that IF produced would be touched by Cattaneo—36 types of automobiles, 18 aero engines, and 19 types of industrial and military vehicles. One of his most significant contributions to the marque, however, was not an automobile. At the 1909 Paris salon, Isotta-Fraschini introduced one of the automotive world's first successful applications of four-wheel brakes, designed and engineered by Cattaneo and Oreste Fraschini.

Following World War I, Isotta-Fraschini embarked upon its greatest era with Oreste Fraschini directing the company's new post-war marketing and design strategies. The prewar years had seen a flurry of Isotta models and the firm's continued support and involvement in motorsports competition. The new Isotta policy would be to offer a single model with the emphasis on luxury and elegance.

The new Isotta, the Tipo 8, was introduced in August 1919. Until World War I, IF had only built four-cylinder engines for its production cars. Cattaneo's new inline eight was the first of its type put into series production anywhere in the world and, of course, the car also offered four-wheel brakes—still not used by virtually anyone else.

*One of the great Italian marques, Isotta-Fraschini reached the zenith of its career with the 8A SS. This 1930 example, bodied as a Cabriolet by Castagna, is typical of the coachmaker's styling, featuring the very costly Grebel headlights and spotlight. The car is now part of the Noel Thompson collection.*

The Tipo 8 engine was a 90-horsepower, overhead-valve, monobloc design displacing 5,890 cubic centimeters (359.4 cubic inches) with an 85x130-millimeter bore and stroke. A by-product of Cattaneo's aircraft engine designs, the Tipo 8 benefited from that technology by using a single-casting aluminum block, steel-lined cylinders, and aluminum pistons.

Oreste Fraschini's new philosophy proved itself right, especially in America, where the Isotta continued to grow in popularity among the well-to-do; not only on the East Coast, where the cars had been well established for years, but in Hollywood. The movie colony found the stylish Isottas more desirable than either Mercedes or Benz models, both of which were still suffering from anti-German sentiment after the war.

Sadly, Oreste Fraschini would not live to see the great Tipo 8 models that would come in the 1920s and 1930s; he died in 1921. And not long after, his brothers and brother-in-law left the company, which was acquired by Count Lodovico Mazzotti. To his credit and good fortune, the Count followed the dictum established by Oreste Fraschini, and he kept Giustino Cattaneo as managing director.

Isotta-Fraschini had established itself as one of the world's most desirable automobiles by the 1920s. Names on the firm's pres-

tigious list of clients included the kings of Italy (Victor Emmanuel) and Iraq (Faisal), the Queen of Romania, the Empress of Abyssinia, Prince Louis of Monaco, the Maharajahs of Alwar and Patiala, and the Aga Kahn. In America, Clara Bow, Jack Dempsey, newspaper publisher William Randolph Hearst, and film star Rudolph Valentino had all become Isotta owners.

With the new Tipo 8A series, horsepower was increased to 110 at 2,400 rpm. Cattaneo also redesigned the frame and suspension, widening the side members, improving the suspension geometry and semi-elliptic springs. The transmission utilized a three-speed, synchromesh unit-construction gearbox or an optional Wilson-type four-speed pre-selector.

Almost in concert with the Tipo 8A's debut, IF introduced the 8A S (*Spinto* or sports) version, which produced 135 horsepower at 2,600 rpm, and the 8A SS (*Super Spinto*), delivering a stunning 160 horsepower and a guaranteed top speed of 100 miles per hour.

Although the Tipo 8 models were large, luxurious touring cars by design, Isotta-Fraschinis performed admirably in competition. Fitted with lightweight, sporting coachwork designed by Carlo Felice Bianchi Anderloni of Touring Superleggera, the Tipo 8

*The Isotta-Fraschini eight-cylinder engine was as beautiful as the bodies designed by Castagna. Under the hood of the Super Spinto, output was a stunning 160 horsepower, and even a Cabriolet was guaranteed a top speed of 100 miles per hour.*

recorded numerous victories in 1921 and 1922 in both touring class and hill-climb competition. Isottas continued to compete throughout the 1920s with an 8A SS winning its class and finishing sixth overall in the 1927 Mille Miglia.

Even though the IF factory continued to downplay motorsports competition (as had been the wishes of Oreste Fraschini), it was difficult not to take note of the Mille Miglia victory, since Count Mazzotti, Isotta's chief executive officer, was among the founders of the classic 1,000-mile race! Still, the image of IF in the 1920s and 1930s was to be *grand luxe*, as was the price.

In America, where nearly a third of the classic era Isottas were sold, a chassis alone was priced at $9,750, and coachbuilt Isottas were demanding upwards of $20,000. In 1930, an Isotta-Fraschini cost more than a Model J Duesenberg.

The cars were treated to an investiture of coachwork by Europe's leading design studios. Carrozzeria Italiana Cesare Sala and Castagna were responsible for the majority of bodies built for the Tipo 8 series, with most of the balance accounted for by Stabilimenti Farina and Touring in Italy, Gurney Nutting, Hooper, and Lancefield in England, and Fleetwood in the United States.

Of all the Italian coachbuilders, the Castagna brothers' designs for Isotta-Fraschini were the most dramatic. Nearly all were done by Emilio Castagna, who excelled in his selection of the finest (if not unique) materials. Ercole Castagna was not beyond going out of house to secure patent rights for specific designs his brother chose to use. One such item was a hood designed by Hibbard and Darrin of Paris; another was the almost exclusive use of French-built Stephen Grebel lights. Interior appointments, fabrics, wood, cabinetry, and the subtle complementing of colors, shapes, and textures were Castagna trademarks.

In all, Tipo 8 production from 1919 to 1924 was 400 cars; Tipo 8A (S and SS) production added up to 950 cars from 1925 to 1931; and just 20 examples of the Tipo 8B were built between 1931 and 1933, when the main factory in Via Monterosa began producing only aero engines. The Depression hit IF very hard, considering its largest market was the United States. With virtually no automobile sales and only aircraft engines being built, IF was sold in 1933 to aircraft manufacturer Count Caproni di Taliedo, and both Mazzotti and Cattaneo took their leave.

Isotta-Fraschini attempted a return to automobile manufacturing after World War II, but the road which these great cars had once traveled no longer existed. The Isotta, like the classic era itself, had became part of the irrevocable past.

# Chapter Five

# British Classics— Rolls-Royce, Bentley, and Company

*The Best of Great Britain*

Proper. That is how most English would have described their cars in the 1920s and 1930s, unless, of course, they were driving a Jaguar, AC, or MG—sporting cars, but hardly proper. There were, however, a handful of English auto makers who managed to combine the best attributes of both, but none more successfully than Walter Owen Bentley.

For those whose automotive passions tend to follow roads less traveled, there is nothing quite the equal of a "vintage" Bentley. Among so many memorable automobiles from the 1920s, these massive steel and fabric-bodied pre-Rolls-Royce Bentleys must stand in any list of the greatest cars ever built. The term "vintage" is used to differentiate models produced by W.O. Bentley as a sovereign manufacturer prior to the purchase of his firm by Rolls-Royce in 1931.

To Bentley purists, this stalwart line of motorcars produced from 1921 to 1931 are the only real Bentleys, cars rich in heritage and unadulterated in their temperament. The W.O. Bentleys were bold, powerful machines, not meant for the weak of motoring spirit. Perhaps that is why author Ian Fleming chose the supercharged "Blower Bentley" as the private transport of his fictional secret agent, James Bond. Yes, it was behind the wheel of a W.O.-era Bentley, not an Aston-Martin and certainly not a BMW, in which Fleming first envisioned 007. Film buffs may recall the Blower Bentley in the

---

*Considered to be one of the world's most beautiful cars, the uniquely styled Lancefield Concealed Drophead Coupe was built for display at the 1938 Motor Show at Earls Court. Unlike most designs of the era which were very rounded, Lancefield chose to use sharp, chiseled styling and a repeating theme running from the front fenders to the rear, into the deck lid, and around the solid boot.*

*Another luxurious alternative to Rolls-Royce, although in a lighter vein, was the Alvis Speed 25. One of the best engineered British automobiles of the 1930s, the Alvis was treated to a variety of body designs by Charlesworth, Van den Plas, Mayfair Carriage Co., Cross & Ellis, and Lancefield. The four-passenger Tourer (red car) was a standard body style produced for Alvis by Charlesworth, Van den Plas, and Cross & Ellis. The two-tone Speed 25 Concealed Drophead Coupe is a one-off design created for Alvis by Lancefield. A near duplicate of this body was also produced in 1936 for the Mercedes-Benz 540K chassis.*

opening scenes of the first Bond film, *Dr. No.* That was in 1962, and at the time more than 30 years had passed since the Bentley name had been independent of Rolls-Royce, yet Fleming recognized the greatness of the W.O. cars long before they were discovered by the collector market.

Back in August 1919, W.O. Bentley had set out with little more than an idea when he formed the small company bearing his name. The Bentley organization began without a factory, without a showroom, and with only one experimental model in existence. Wrote historian Ken Purdy, "On this slippery foundation, W.O. Bentley and his associates, a devoted lot indeed, erected a company that lasted for only twelve years and in that short time made itself immortal in the history of the trade." Immortality in the automotive world, however, is hard-earned, and most of the auto makers who achieved it did so by failing rather than succeeding. Bentley managed to do both.

W.O.'s timing was perhaps not as good as that of his engines, entering into the automotive field in the weak post-World War I economy with one of the most expensive cars on the British market. It was also one of the best.

Bentley was a designer of formidable competence. A competitor on motorcycles and in race cars, he had a keen understanding for the demands competition placed on an automobile's engine, suspension, and chassis. The cars W.O. produced were suited equally to London roadways or the Mulsanne straight at Le Mans, where Bentleys were triumphant in 1924, and again in 1927, 1928, 1929, and 1930, a record unmatched until the 1950s.

In his youth, W.O. had apprenticed with the Great Northern Railway, developing a passion for steam locomotives that prevailed throughout his life. It is said he brought too much of his love for locomotives into the design of the Bentley chassis, a massive steelwork structure that was built well beyond its needs. But strength

*One of the most popular Alvis body styles, the four-passenger Tourer was handsomely designed by Charlesworth with rakish cut-down doors, skirted front fenders, and side mount spares. The Speed 25 Tourer was considered a contemporary of the SS 100 Jaguar.*

was a Bentley characteristic, both in the man and his cars. And it was that strength which enabled a Bentley 3-liter driven by S.C.H. Davis to survive the "Crash at White House Corner" and continue on to victory at Le Mans in 1927.

The famous collision happened well into the race, at around 9:30 P.M. with two 3-liter Bentleys and one 4 1/2 liter model competing for the lead. As the trio came into White House Corner, they encountered a French Schneider spun out across the road. Leslie Cunningham, driving the 4 1/2-liter at almost 80 miles per hour, left the road rather than broadside the Schneider, but damaged his car beyond repair. George Duller followed Cunningham in a 3-liter, choosing to drive his car off the course as well. Having witnessed the fate of his teammates, Davis tried to maneuver around the Schneider. That didn't work either. Sustaining heavy damage from the impact, the Bentley limped back to the pits with a badly bent front axle, a broken wheel, cracked steering-arm joint, broken headlights, and smashed fenders. Still mechanically sound, the car was patched up and sent back into competition. At midnight, co-driver J.D. Benjafield took over from Davis, manhandling the 3-liter throughout the night and on to victory. Had there been any reservations about the strength of the Bentley chassis or the reliability of its components, Le Mans certainly assuaged any doubt.

Although financed well enough to continue development of new engines and chassis, Bentley's sales were never brisk. Early Bentley owners were mostly enthusiastic young sportsmen, "The Bentley Boys," as they came to be known in racing circles—the biggest group of men ever to find prominence in motorsports merely by driving one marque. Victories from the Tourist Trophy Race to Le Mans helped establish the company as Great Britain's equal to Mercedes. However, unlike Mercedes, which sold more cars because of its racing image, Bentley's competition successes seemed to work more against the company than in its favor. Many who could afford the cars were afraid to buy them believing that only a race driver could handle a Bentley. That the very same cars which had won Le Mans could as easily be smooth and silent boulevard carriages did not wrest the image of W.O.'s massive tourers as dusty, oil-stained, top-down racers. Indeed they were among the first genuine *gran turismos* of the era, cars that paved the way for future generations of sporting convertibles and sedans, but in the 1920s, Bentleys were more often the object of distant admiration.

Even with financing from millionaire sportsman Woolf "Babe" Barnato—the most prominent of the "Bentley Boys" and three-time winner at Le Mans—the company was never sufficiently profitable, and Barnato's help had come at the expense of W.O.'s control. After 1925, Barnato became chairman of the reorganized Bentley Motors, Ltd., and when the company finally went into receivership in June 1931, in debt even beyond Barnato's ability or desire to continue, Bentley could do nothing to prevent the company from being sold. Expecting a friendly takeover by an organization named British Central Equitable Trust, Ltd., Bentley was shocked to learn that British Central was a front for Rolls-Royce. W.O. Bentley suddenly found himself an employee of what ostensibly had been his chief rival for nearly a decade. When his contract with Rolls-Royce came up for renewal in 1935, Bentley left to join Lagonda, where he would remain as technical director for 11 years.

*Among the last of the W.O. Bentley-era cars built at Cricklewood, this 1931 Eight Liter was bodied by Barker as a Boattail Speedster with dickey seat, the only known use of this body style on an Eight Liter chassis. A similar body was mounted on a Speed Six chassis for the 1929 London Motor Show. The most powerful of the W.O. cars, the Eight Liter in-line six-cylinder engine had four valves per cylinder, eight main bearings, and a single overhead camshaft driven by three concentric rods at the back of the engine. Bentley chose this over conventional gear or chain drive methods because it allowed for a smoother and quieter running engine. The Bentley Eight developed up to 250 horsepower, considerably more than the Rolls-Royce Phantom II with which it competed. Reason enough for R-R to purchase the company.*

Although Bentleys were intended for owners with far more brio than those who usually confined themselves to the extravagantly crafted rear compartments of Rolls-Royces, the prestigious British auto maker considered Bentley an important acquisition. The Bentley was a driver's car, something Rolls-Royce did not generally produce. A new company was formed after 1931, Bentley Motors, Ltd., which became a wholly-owned subsidiary of Rolls-Royce. The first new model was the 3 1/2-liter introduced in 1933, for which the phrase "The Silent Sports Car" was coined. And it is here at this juncture that purists separate vintage Bentleys from those which followed under the Rolls-Royce standard.

*One of the most attractive Rolls-Royce Bentley models of the late 1930s, this one-off Airflow Saloon was built in 1936 on the 4-1/4 Liter chassis. Designed by Gurney-Nutting chief stylist A. F. McNeill, the sleek, fastback four-door sedan was among a handful of trend-setting cars of similar design built in Europe and the United States throughout the mid- to late 1930s. The fastback style would be continued by automotive designers well into the post-World War II era.*

For the better part of Bentley history, the cars which bore the winged B were simply known by numbers denoting their engine displacement in liters, a rudimentary formula that W.O. found satisfactory. He was a man dedicated to engineering the best motorcar England or the world had ever seen up to that time, and along the way, he produced a handful of remarkable automobiles.

Bentley began with a 3-liter, four-cylinder design in 1922 and continued to produce variants of the 3-liter models through 1931. A short-chassis 3-liter appeared in 1924, known as the "speed model." It was capable of 100-mile-per-hour stretches and had surprising power and acceleration, as witnessed by the competition in the 1924 Le Mans race. The 4 1/2-liter models arrived in 1927 and supercharged versions were introduced in 1929. The proportion of blown to unblown Bentley 4 1/2s was 54 to 1,620. And for W.O. that was 54 too many.

Building a supercharged version of the 4 1/2 was not Bentley's decision. It was at the behest of company financier Woolf Barnato

who, having been convinced of the advantages of supercharging by factory race driver Sir Henry "Tim" Birkin, backed production of the blown engines. Bentley felt that to supercharge one of his cars would, to use his own words, "pervert its design and corrupt its performance," and his beliefs were later substantiated when the majority of blown Bentleys failed under extreme use. When the first engine was tested for maximum power, it was found to be producing 240 horsepower at 4,200 rpm, an 80-percent increase over the unblown model, and a sure sign that reliability problems were only as far away as the first race. As a team, the supercharged cars were entered in a total of 10 races, but victory always eluded the Blower Bentleys. Though new lap records were consistently established, breakdowns involving the valve gear were frequent and mechanical failure plagued the cars from the start. The best finish ever for a blown 4 1/2 was the 1930 French Grand Prix, when a two-ton Bentley four-seater trounced all but one of a first-rate field of GP cars. Supercharged Bentleys finished third in the Irish GP of 1929, and fourth in 1930, otherwise they broke, crashed, or finished well back.

As a road car, the Blower Bentley was a truly impressive automobile, and for short stints problems were seldom encountered, as owners usually ran out of road or nerve before the Bentley engine ran out of power. As a competition car, however, it was an imperfect design, which enjoyed neither the vast experience of the Bentley factory, having been built in a separate facility, nor the blessings of the man whose name it bore. Nevertheless, it did nothing to tarnish the Bentley reputation. At worst, it created an element of doubt about the reliability of Bentley motorcars.

In the *Illustrated History of the Bentley Car,* W.O. commented that the blown models "...gave us all a good deal of additional anxiety during our already anxious last months... it cost us a great deal of goodwill, because the supercharged cars lacked the steady reliability which had, from the beginning, been part of Bentley Motor's religion. The 'blowers' also added to the slightly suspect 'fast-living' connotations associated with the marque..."

Even in normally aspirated form, the Bentley 4 1/2 was an impressive automobile. With a 100x140-millimeter bore and stroke, four valves per cylinder driven by a single overhead camshaft, dual magnetos and spark plugs, a five-bearing crank, and integral block and cylinder head, it was an almost indestructible engine until Birkin had Charles Amherst Villiers add the Roots-type blower.

In the end, however, Bentley had to agree that the attraction of the supercharged engine was undeniable. He later wrote, "...the magic of the supercharger was not yet dimmed. No one could resist its lure... and, of course, they were very fast while they lasted." The 4 1/2-liter Bentleys, blown or otherwise, have indeed lasted to become one of the marque's most-coveted automobiles and the quintessential vintage Bentley.

The larger six-cylinder 6 1/2-liter cars, manufactured from 1926 to 1930, were intended for more-formal coachwork, although many were as rakishly bodied as the sporting "Speed Six" series. Along with the massive new Eight Liter six-cylinder models introduced in 1930, these were the first Bentleys to come into direct competition with Rolls-Royce, particularly the Phantom I and Phantom II.

W.O. had actually gone up against Rolls-Royce when he introduced the Bentley Eight Liter chassis in 1930. The majority of cars were fitted with very formal coachwork, and for the first time Bentleys were truly encroaching on Rolls-Royce turf. W.O. had even priced the Eight Liter at a shade over that of the new Rolls-Royce Phantom II. This may well have been the reason R-R so actively pursued the purchase of Bentley in 1931. By that time more than 100 Eight Liter chassis had been produced, of which 62 had already been delivered to coachbuilders. In all, the prestigious H.J. Mulliner works had built 23 Bentley bodies, Thrupp & Maberly 14, Freestone & Webb 13, Park Ward 5, Vanden Plas 8, and even Gurney Nutting—one of R-R's preeminent coachbuilders—produced 13 bodies for the Bentley Eight.

*One of the hallmarks of W.O. Bentley's career was the 4-1/2 Liter Touring. The cars were mostly fabric-bodied, like this 1929 example from the William B. Ruger, Sr., collection. In normally aspirated form, the Bentley 4-1/2 was an impressive automobile. The Bentley six-cylinder was an almost indestructible engine mounted to an equally indestructible steel chassis. Although somewhat harsh-riding, the Bentley's rock-solid suspension endowed the cars with superior handling ability, proven in race after race by essentially the very same cars offered for sale to the public.*

By the end of 1931, the big Bentleys had also been treated to coachwork by Letourneur et Marchand, Kellner, Binder, and Saoutchik in France, and one had even been delivered to the United States to be fitted with a body by Duesenberg's principal coachbuilder, Walter M. Murphy.

Among a handful of exceptional bodies produced for the last of the W.O. Bentleys was a Barker Boattail built in 1931. It was ordered by Sir P. Malcolm Stewart and built on the 144-inch short-wheelbase Eight Liter chassis. The handsome speedster body was done in the traditional Labourdette Skiff style, that of an upright hull, which creates a deck aft of the driver's compartment, providing space for a very large and easily entered rumble or dickey seat. Measuring almost 17 feet from bumper to bumper, the Barker was a massive automobile with the two-passenger driving compartment positioned at the center of the body. The stunning Barker Boattail was among the last of the W.O. Bentleys.

The acquisition of Bentley was probably a wise move on the part of Rolls-Royce. Had the Bentley name and designs gone to

*When W.O. Bentley left Rolls-Royce in 1935, he crossed over from Derby to Middlesex taking a position as chief engineer at Lagonda, a company that had for years been a competitor to the sporting Bentley models. The first model to be breathed upon by W.O. was the 1936 LG45 Rapide Tourer. The 1937 model pictured carries a body designed by stylist Frank Feeley who used every contemporary styling cliche in the book for the LG45. The Rapide Tourer deliberately capitalized on Bentley styling for the grille and hood line, but Feeley pulled out all the stops with raked fender lines, a narrow fuselage accentuated by severely cut-down doors, and massive flex-pipe exhausts. It was a design guaranteed to attract attention anywhere it was driven.*

*The American Rolls-Royce Phantom, known as the Springfield Rolls-Royce, was a left-hand-drive version introduced in 1926, replacing the American-built Ghost, and produced through 1931. The Phantom I was brought out in 1925 to replace the British Silver Ghost built from 1907. The Phantom I was a transitional model and carried coachwork similar to the later Ghosts until new styles appeared in 1928 and 1929. The car pictured is a 1928 Springfield model known as an Ascot Dual Cowl Phaeton. The Ascot is considered to be one of the most collectible of the Springfield Phantoms.*

another of its competitors, the very future of Rolls-Royce may have been altered. The Bentley was a substantially more powerful automobile, and with handling and ride comfort equal to that of the Phantom II, an overall better car for the money. It was also too expensive to manufacture, and Rolls-Royce did not continue Eight Liter production in 1932. Instead, the Rolls-Royce Bentley was built on a modified 20/25 chassis and equipped with a slightly more powerful version of the Rolls-Royce 3 1/2-liter engine. Its successor, the 4 1/4 Bentley, used the 25/30 Rolls-Royce engine and was built from 1936 to 1939. The great individuality that had separated Bentley from Rolls-Royce was reduced to a difference in grilles, trim, coachwork, and perhaps intent, as Bentley was marketed as a sportier car than the Rolls-Royce.

Under Rolls-Royce, Bentley coachwork probably improved over that of the W.O. line as Bentley chassis were now being sent to the same coachbuilders as Rolls-Royce. Bodies by Gurney Nutting, one of the leading design firms in all of Great Britain, were suddenly more conspicuous on Bentley chassis, which were sporting trend-setting coachwork by chief stylist A.F. McNeill.

In 1929, McNeill had been commissioned by Woolf Barnato to design a special body for the Bentley Speed Six chassis. McNeill's

design built by Gurney Nutting was to become the most famous Bentley ever produced, the legendary Blue Train. A close second, for sheer flamboyance of line and form, was a 4 1/4 chassis bodied by McNeill and Gurney Nutting in 1936 as an Airflow Saloon. Translated into English that would be an Aerodynamic Sedan. As someone once said, "The Americans and the British are two people separated by a common language."

By the mid-1930s, the era of aerodynamics was coming into its own and coachbuilders throughout Europe and the United States were beginning to experiment with fastback designs, although literally cheating the wind was far less of an imperative at the time than giving the appearance of having done so.

In America, the fastback look first appeared between 1933 and 1936. Cadillac was the first, introducing the Fleetwood-designed V-16 Aero-Dynamic Coupe at the 1933 Chicago Century of Progress Exposition. Duesenberg stylist J. Herbert Newport penned a sport coupe built by Walker-LaGrande in 1934. At Packard, a similar though more daring design was evolving, which led to the 1934 Model 1106 Sport Coupes. In Pasadena, California coachbuilder Bohman and Schwartz built the Mudd Coupe in 1936 with lines similar to both the 1934 Packard and the 1935 Mercedes-Benz

*The Rolls-Royce Phantom II was introduced in September 1929. A revised engine design increased output to around 120 horsepower at 3,000 rpm. Later Phantom II engines managed 158 horsepower with a higher 5.25:1 compression ratio and a different carburetor. Produced through 1935, the body styles offered on the Phantom II marked the high point in prewar Rolls-Royce coachwork. This AJS chassis was built in England with left-hand-drive for export to the United States. The car was delivered to Brewster & Co. in New York City for coachwork. Brewster had been building bodies for Rolls-Royce in the United States since 1908, and produced nearly all of the coachwork for the Springfield Silver Ghosts and Phantoms.*

*The "Countess" is the most famous Rolls-Royce Phantom II built. At one of Clark Gable's parties, designer Howard "Dutch" Darrin, who had built several custom-bodied cars for the actor, met the Countess Dorothy di Frasso. As Darrin later recalled, "The Countess was a great rival of actress star Constance Bennett, although they were warm personal friends, they always tried to outdo one another. Miss Bennett had a special-bodied Rolls-Royce with a canework passenger compartment and it really bugged the Countess not to have something equally elegant." Countess di Frasso handed Darrin the keys to her 1933 Phantom II limousine and asked him to rebody it into something that would rival Bennett's Phantom II. Darrin began in 1936 and it took two years to complete the car. The fastback body was made of aluminum and designed with an enclosed rear compartment featuring a duplicate of the rakishly angled split front windshield.*

The lines of the "Countess" are typical of town car designs
although, as wielded by Darrin, exaggerated to give the car
unique character with the fastback appearance in vogue
during the late 1930s. The hood is one of the longest ever,
placing the driving compartment behind the half-way point of
the chassis. The rear compartment is luxuriously appointed
but intended to seat only two. The split windshield can also
be cranked down into the divider.

500K Autobahn Kurier exhibited at the Berlin Auto Show. While all of these examples were trend-setting designs, none had either the fluidity of line or the dignified propriety of McNeill's 1936 4 1/4-liter Airflow Saloon.

When W.O. Bentley took his leave from Rolls-Royce in 1935, his first post-R-R efforts turned up under the hood of a Lagonda, another company Rolls-Royce had wanted to acquire in order to eliminate the competition. This time, however, it was outbid by a wealthy young solicitor named Alan Good, who paid £71,000 for Lagonda, taking the company from its receivers in 1935. It was Good who also secured the services of W.O. Bentley, another slap at Rolls-Royce.

Originally an independent company, Lagonda was one of England's oldest automotive marques, a name steeped in tradition, punctuated with historic figures, and embossed with a torrid and chaotic past.

Although a British company, Lagonda's founder Wilber Gunn was an American who emigrated to England from Ohio before the turn of the century. He had grown up near the Lagonda river, and took the name for his company.

Gunn began, as did so many in the early 1900s, by building a simple, single-cylinder engine with which to power a three-wheeled carriage. Early on, Lagonda subsisted from year to year by producing tiny quantities of superbly built motorcars. Following his death in 1920, the company's managing body kept Lagonda on the road, expanding slowly into the late 1920s and early 1930s, always on the ragged edge, occasionally over it, and into the rescuing hands of a procession of owners.

Lagonda designs have ranged from the single-cylinder 3-wheeled carriages of 1906, to models powered by two-, four-, and six-cylinder motors, and finally the Bentley-designed twelve.

The greatest prewar Lagonda was the 1936-1937 LG45 Rapide designed by Dick Watney, managing director of Lagonda under new owner Alan Good, or more appropriately, in the turbulent history of the Stains, Middlesex, auto maker, the debtor in possession.

Watney believed that Lagonda was in need of a car such as this, one which would stir the blood of British manhood and challenge the 500K *Reichwagen* of Daimler-Benz. Thus, the new Lagonda Good works set about building an out-and-out sports car on a shoestring budget.

The foundation for the Rapide was patterned on the earlier M45R, which had been successfully campaigned in the 1935 24 Heures du Mans and Tourist Trophy races.

With new operating capital, a trio of LG45 Rapides were developed from 1935 to 1938, each distinctively different in styling. The first was a classic close-coupled, four-passenger open body on a special short 123-inch wheelbase chassis powered by a 4 1/2-liter overhead-valve (ohv) six designed by Henry Meadows. It was the same basic engine used in the championship Le Mans race cars. The second Rapide version with a Tourer body appeared in 1936, powered by a 4 1/2-liter six overhauled by Bentley, who became Lagonda's technical director in June 1935. The third and last Rapide model was brought to market in 1938, and featured a convertible body style. Of the three versions, the second was the most outstanding, and one of the most sensational British automobiles of the era.

The body design for the 1936-1937 Rapide was delegated to stylist Frank Feeley, a man whose talents ranged from the mundane to the inspired. The Rapide Tourer managed to evoke both extremes. In many ways it was not unlike a Bentley in appearances, Feeley having captured something of that look in front. For what it's worth, if you compare the Bentley emblem and grille with that of Lagonda's, there is a striking resemblance in their design, which was no coincidence. Feeley completed the design with bold, arched fenders surrounding a narrow fuselage, accentuated by severely cut-down doors. Deeply relieved moldings, running aft from the grille shell, through the hood, over the cowl, and along the length of the doors, further highlighted the Rapide's sweeping symmetry.

From almost any forward view, the car exhibited sharp, cutting lines, further enhanced on the left side by a pair of chrome-plated flex pipes passing through the hood panel and disappearing beneath the running board. At the rear, the Lagonda had a short trunk which provided a cache for both the spare tire and fuel tank.

The all-aluminum bodies were built at the Lagonda factory and fitted to the LG45's 129-inch-wheelbase chassis. The pushrod ohv six beneath the hood displaced 272.5 cubic inches, with a bore and stroke of 3.50x4.75 inches and an output of 150 horsepower. The four-main-bearing engine used two SU carburetors and one Vertex magneto. Delivering its *puissance* through a massive 4-speed synchromesh gearbox, the Bentley-designed engine could take the Rapide to a maximum speed of 100 miles per hour at 4,000 rpm. With a curb weight of 3,557 pounds, the Lagonda could accelerate from rest to 60 miles per hour in 13.1 seconds and turn the quarter-mile in 19 seconds at 72 miles per hour. Sensational stuff in 1937.

In all, Lagonda built only 25 LG45 Rapide Tourers, 24 of which are still known to exist. The Tourer was by design one of the sportiest cars ever produced by Lagonda.

In 1947, Good sold out to David Brown, following Brown's purchase of another financially destitute British company, Aston-Martin. The resulting amalgamation, Aston Martin Lagonda, became one of the most recognized names in the automotive world with the introduction of the DB series, and another victory at Le Mans in 1959 with American driver Carroll Shelby. Today, Aston Martin Lagonda is a subsidiary of Ford Motor Company.

Up against historic figures like Frederick Henry Royce, Charles Stewart Rolls, and Walter Owen Bentley, T.G. John is hardly a prestigious name in the British auto industry. However, in 1919 Thomas George John bought his way into automotive history by purchasing the Holley Brothers carburetor manufacturing plant in Coventry, England, along with G.P.H. de Freville's plans for a 10/30-horsepower auto called the Alvis.

The Alvis owed its uniqueness to de Freville, who used aluminum in the design for his pistons and coined the Alvis name from the chemical symbol for aluminum, AL, and the Latin for strength, VIS. Thus, Alvis was born out of aluminum, strength, and T.G. John's money in July 1920.

John understood marketing, but what he didn't know about engineering could have filled volumes. He was wise enough, however, to surround himself with people who made up for his lack of mechanical ability. When the de Freville design had problems, John hired designer/engineer Captain George Thomas Smith-Clarke, assistant works manager with Daimler, Ltd., who quickly took command of the Alvis factory and put things in order. John could have employed a full-time patent attorney to keep up with Smith-Clarke's

*Even more outrageous than Darrin's design for the Countess di Frasso is this 1932 Rolls-Royce Phantom II bodied in France by Figoni et Falaschi as a Pillarless Sedan. Possibly the most extraordinary body ever built for a Rolls-Royce, Figoni used the same styling as he would on a Delahaye, Delage, or Talbot-Lago. Scaled up to fit the massive 150-inch Phantom II wheelbase, the sleek fastback proportions are equally as stunning. But Figoni outdid himself on the pillarless door design, which allows the almost seamless reverse-hinged doors to open away from each other providing complete access into both the front and rear compartments.*

inventions. A man who considered safety his first responsibility, Smith-Clarke almost went too far in manufacturing reliability into the Alvis. For example, the oil pan on the 1936 Speed 25 model was held in place by 38 bolts. He simultaneously pioneered independent front suspension and front-wheel-drive for the Alvis racing cars, and patented more than 100 features used on Alvis models, rendering them the most solid and reliable British cars of the 1920s and 1930s.

During the 1930s it was John's decision to move Alvis into the luxury car field with models such as the Speed 20 and Speed 25,

automobiles that were very close to Rolls-Royce and Bentley quality. The Speed 20 engine, like its designer, Smith-Clarke, was quite unconventional. An inline six with two overhead valves per cylinder actuated by pushrods and rockers, the engine featured a detachable head, Alvis-patented multiple valve springs, and a four-main-bearing crankshaft. The camshaft, magneto, coil distributor, generator, and water pump were driven off the *rear* of the engine.

*The Lancefield body for Alvis was actually a copy of one done in 1936 for a Mercedes-Benz 540K chassis. The 540K was rarely seen with anything but a Sindelfingen body, although it is believed Lancefield built two cars in this style on 540K chassis.*

---

Another of Smith-Clarke's inventions was the first four-speed all-synchromesh gearbox used in any production automobile. It was introduced on the 1934 Alvis Speed 20. The improved Speed 25, with a seven-main-bearing crankshaft engine, Dewandre vacuum servo-assist brakes, and Luvax finger-tip control shock absorbers, were all new features, yet the Speed 25 was priced exactly the same as the model it replaced.

John chose the finest coachbuilders in England to design and produce bodies for the Alvis chassis, including Charlesworth, which John had controlling interest in from 1936 on. Charlesworth was responsible for mostly traditional coachwork, such as the four-passenger tourer. When something more flamboyant was required, John turned to the coachbuilders at Lancefield.

Producing some of the most attractive and avant-garde bodies of the late 1930s, Lancefield had been in the coachwork trade since 1922, when it opened under the name Gaisford and Warboys, owned and operated by Harry, Edwin, and Bob Gaisford and George Warboys. By 1936, when the firm created the stylish Concealed Drophead Coupe design used on the Alvis Speed 25, Mercedes-Benz 540K, Rolls-Royce Phantom, Bentley, and Hotchkiss chassis, the firm employed over 60 skilled craftsmen. "Of all the cars my brothers and I designed," wrote 85-year-old Bob Gaisford in 1983, "the Concealed Drophead Coupe was my favorite."

Like Alvis, Lancefield went into aircraft production during World War II. Both of their factories were destroyed by the *Blitzkrieg*. Lancefield rebuilt but finally closed its doors in 1972. A decade later Gaisford was honored by the *Autoshow der Superlative-Veedol Starparade* held in Berlin for having produced one of the world's most beautiful cars, the Alvis Speed 25 Concealed Drophead Coupe.

Alvis continued postwar production through 1967, but the company's main business was aero engines and military vehicles. All car production finally ceased in 1967, by which time Alvis had been acquired by British Leyland. In 1971, Alvis was contracted by the British military to build light tanks, the business in which it has been engaged ever since.

# Chapter Six

# Transatlantic Designs— From Paris to Pasadena

## American Cars Bodied in Europe, European Cars Bodied in America

A Bentley bodied in Pasadena, California? A Packard with coachwork executed in London, England? A Duesenberg built in Paris, France? As odd as that may sound, throughout the 1920s and 1930s American- and European-built chassis crossed the Atlantic with clock-like regularity. For the wealthy clientele of the world's greatest motorcar manufacturers, spending thousands more to have a custom body manufactured by a famous coachbuilder was well within their means, even if that coachbuilder was half a world away.

In 1927, a Mercedes-Benz 630 chassis was sent to carrozzeria Castagna in Italy for coachwork, at the request of an American customer. The following year, a Mercedes-Benz SSK chassis was shipped to Pasadena, California, to have a boattail body designed and built by the Walter M. Murphy company. Newspaper publishing tycoon William Randolph Hearst had a Duesenberg chassis shipped to Americans Dutch Darrin and Thomas Hibbard in Paris, France, to have one of

*In 1947, Frenchman E. Gadol of Boulogne had the tenacity to order a British car! He also had the good sense to have the body for the Mk VI Bentley built at the rue du Caporal Peugeot, Paris, Salon of the Franay Brothers. The Bentley was the most advanced chassis Rolls-Royce had to offer after the war. A completely new design, it featured independent front suspension, and the same 4-1/4-liter six-cylinder engine that would power the postwar Rolls-Royce Silver Wraith. England's motoring authority, The Autocar, proclaimed the Mk VI, "...a new thrill which mere words cannot convey. It is a completely docile, silent town car, and a fast touring hill-devouring vehicle rolled into one." The car is currently in the Gary Wales collection.*

their exclusive *Sylentlyte* cast aluminum framed bodies built. For Hearst, H&D produced a striking Transformable Cabriolet, which combined the best features of a phaeton with a luxurious town car. Upon its return to America, Hearst gave the Duesenberg to film star Marion Davies, with whom he carried on a long-time love affair. Davies was so taken with the car that whenever she traveled to Europe with Hearst, they took the Duesenberg with them!

In the 1930s, more Duesenbergs found their way to Europe than any other American marque. It is estimated that 50 Model J chassis were fitted with European coachwork, mostly by the leading French carrosserie. Saoutchik, Figoni et Falaschi, Hibbard & Darrin (later Fernandez & Darrin), Letourneur et Marchand, Labourdette, and Franay, all created designs on American made chassis.

Figoni built the famous "French Speedster" in 1931 on a Model J Duesenberg chassis commissioned by Paris automobile importer E.Z. Sadovich, who sold the car to millionaire industrialist Antonio Chopitea. This is perhaps the best known of all Duesenbergs built in France. In 1932, the Speedster won the Grand Prix award at the Cannes Concours d'Elegance. One of the few occasions when an American chassis was so honored.

While Bentleys were most often bodied in Great Britain, a 1931 Eight Liter chassis was shipped all the way to Pasadena, California, where the Walter M. Murphy Company, known for building Duesenberg bodies, was commissioned to design and manufacture a convertible coupe. Stylist Frank Hershey, best remembered

*The Bentley was displayed on the Franay stand at the 1947 Paris Salon de l'Auto before being delivered to Gadol. On June 12, 1948, he entered the car in the Concours d'Elegance at Enghien and was awarded the Grand Prix in all categories. The following weekend the Bentley appeared at the Bois de Boulogne Concours d'Elegance with the same results. The Gadols are pictured with the car in 1948, which they drove blissfully away from the Concours and enjoyed until they sold it in 1951. It took present owner Gary Wales ten years to restore the car, which was completed in 1991 and shown at the prestigious Pebble Beach Concours d'Elegance, where it won the French Cup. The first time ever that the award has gone to a British car. History repeats itself.*

*The mighty Bentley in-line 8-liter six came from Cricklewood with either a 5:1 compression ratio or optional 5.5:1. Output for the engine ranged from 200 to 230 horsepower, depending on compression and tune. Fuel was delivered through twin SU HO8 carburetors and consumed at the rate of 11.5 miles per gallon. Far more powerful than the Rolls-Royce Phantom II, this was one of the reasons R-R actively sought to purchase Bentley in 1931.*

*In profile, this 1931 Eight Liter Bentley Convertible Coupe bodied by the Walter M. Murphy Co. of Pasadena, California, has little resemblance to typical British-built cars of the era. The lines look more like that of a Duesenberg. Says historian and Murphy authority Strother MacMinn, "The Murphy design has a perfectly balanced set of proportions that make this car as exciting as it is. There's no artificial styling. It's all basic proportions and beautifully done."*

for designing the Ford Thunderbird in 1955, was Murphy's chief stylist back then, and he recalls that the Bentley was ordered by C.H. Matthiessen, Jr., of Santa Barbara, California.

Originally, Hershey's design had been for a sporty four-door convertible sedan along the lines of the Murphy Company's Duesenberg body style, but when the Eight Liter Bentley chassis arrived from England, it was the short 144-inch wheelbase and not the long 156-inch chassis Matthiessen had ordered. The body Hershey had designed wouldn't fit.

Recalls Hershey, "Mr. Matthiessen didn't want to send [the chassis] back to England, so I had to adapt my design to fit." As a result, Hershey and the Murphy Company created one of the most visually stunning two-door convertible coupes ever built.

"There wasn't much fuss over it," says Hershey, now age 89. "I took a couple of days to redesign it and the first drawing was approved." However, according to Hershey, the revised design to

accommodate the shorter wheelbase was not as attractive as the original. "It's just my opinion, but I felt that the body side was too high for a coupe, but Mr. Matthiessen liked it. I would have lowered the door height by another inch or two simply because you can't hang your elbow out of that car," still laments Hershey more than 60 years later.

Historian, author, and automotive designer Strother MacMinn, a long-time friend of Hershey, and a Murphy authority, remembers the car very well. "It had a couple of unique features. One of them was that the body had no beltline. The roll of the hood goes right on through into the body. A perfectly balanced set of proportions that make this car as exciting as it is. There's no artificial styling. It's all basic proportions and beautifully done."

This was something of a Murphy trademark, says MacMinn. "They built a whole slug of convertible sedans, and even though this is a convertible coupe, it has that same stock in trade look about it."

*It was called the "French Speedster," a name that conjures up visions of long-forgotten road races, the Cannes Concours d'Elegance, and elegant social affairs along the Riviera. Images that in the case of this 1931 Model J Duesenberg are all true. Chassis J-465 was ordered by E.Z. Sadovich, the Duesenberg distributor in Paris, and delivered to carrossier Figoni et Falaschi where the French master designer Joseph Figoni created the stunning boattail speedster body. Delivered in the white to Sadovich, he took the unpainted car and entered it in the Paris to Nice rallye in March 1932. As intended, the car caught the attention of Antonio Chopitea, a Peruvian industrialist who spent his summers in France and owned several Model J Duesenbergs. Chopitea purchased the car from Sadovich, had it painted two-tone blue, and then entered it in the August 27 Cannes Concours d'Elegance where it won the Grand Prix. The car is now in the Sam and Emily Mann collection.*

Indeed, at a glance, anyone familiar with classic era coachwork would have to agree that this car bears all of the celebrated Murphy styling cues—long, flowing beaded-edge fenders, lengthy hood line, and a rakishly angled windshield—the trademarks of a Frank Hershey design.

Hershey went to work for Murphy in 1928. Although he left for six months to work in Harley Earl's new Art & Colour Section at GM, he returned when Murphy offered to triple his salary, and he remained there until 1932. Hershey designed more than 40 cars by the time Murphy closed its doors. "Murphy was designing and building bodies for nearly every major American luxury car chassis,"

recalls Hershey, "and business had been good despite the economy after 1929. Then it took a sudden drop in 1932. It wasn't that we didn't have cars to build, but the handwriting was on the wall. Mr. Murphy could have gone on, he had the money, but he decided to get out of the automobile business. And that was that."

According to MacMinn's history on the Murphy Company, the Bentley was originally painted black and was to have featured a new dashboard design Hershey had been working on which placed all of the instruments behind one piece of painted glass, rather than using a traditional fascia with individual gauges mounted through it. For some reason it was never done on the Bentley, but appeared later on Her-

*The massive flex pipes used on supercharged Model J exhausts became a trend-setting design of the 1930s. The bold, polished exhaust tubes became so popular that Duesenberg owners who did not have supercharged models sent their cars back to the factory to have the stylish new cut-out hood panels and exhaust system fitted to their cars. Custom coachbuilders such as Bohman & Schwartz also fitted non-supercharged cars with blower-style exhausts.*

shey's design for the 1932 Peerless V-16 prototype, which by no small coincidence has fenderlines and taillights identical to the Bentley.

Another feature unique for a Bentley, but common for a Murphy design, was the use of all-metal construction, which the Pasadena firm had begun using in 1930. Says MacMinn, "this is one reason why this car survived, because so little wood was used in its construction."

The most distinguishing feature of the Murphy-bodied Bentley was that it didn't look British. If not for the grille, it could well have been a Duesenberg. "The Murphy Convertible Coupe had flowing body lines. In general, British coachwork appeared a bit more cumbersome back then, very perpendicular," says Hershey.

It was for that very reason—the staid, formal styling that the British coachbuilders were known for—that Canadian liquor distiller Harry C. Hatch commissioned the House of Barker, coachbuilder to Rolls-Royce and the Royal Family, to build the Sedanca de Ville body for his 1938 Packard. The man behind Hiram Walker-Gooderham & Worts, Ltd. of Canada, Hatch could afford any car in the world, but he chose Packards for their mechanical reliability; however, he preferred British coachwork. Unless one sees the stately Packard Super-Eight grille and hood line, the Sedanca de Ville appears to be a Rolls-Royce.

Hatch found Barker's dignified and traditional styling very appealing. His Packard looked like a car built for the Royal Family, and the craftsmen at Barker expended the same amount of effort, sparing no expense on the all-aluminum, chauffeured limousine body, hand-crafted interior, luxury fabrics, and appointments. The car even had a built-in safe for storing valuables.

Fit for a king, a queen, or a liquor baron, the Sedanca de Ville was simply enormous, especially when viewed from the rear with the high formal roofline. As traditional as any Rolls-Royce could be, except that this was a Packard.

Sometimes the design characteristics of an individual manufacturer are so dominating that even foreign coachwork cannot change the image of the car. This was the case in 1928 when another Santa Barbara resident, Howard Isham, decided to have the Walter M. Murphy Co. build a boattail speedster for a Mercedes-Benz SSK chassis.

When you think about boattail speedsters, images of sporty two-seat Auburns and Duesenbergs dressed in sweeping coachwork with narrow tapered tails come to mind; racy cars that appealed to youthful, well-monied drivers throughout the 1920s and 1930s. However, one would be hard pressed to picture this type of body on an SSK chassis.

As far as can be determined, only one SSK Boattail Speedster was ever built, and of the entire SSK production, roughly 31 cars, only two were bodied outside of Europe and Great Britain; the second, also by Murphy, was a cabriolet built for actor Zeppo Marx. Several S, SS, and SSK chassis were bodied outside of Germany, mainly in France by Saoutchik, in England by Freestone and Webb, and in Italy by Castagna.

Given the dazzling character of the Mercedes-Benz grille, the enormous trio of exhaust tubes streaming from the hood panel, and the boldly exposed semi-elliptical frame rails and leaf springs protruding beyond the front apron, there was nothing Murphy could do to change the car's appearance forward of the cowl. Little wonder Murphy stylists paid so much attention to the passenger compartment and design of the rear deck.

Perhaps the raciest looking SSK ever built, the Murphy Boattail was literally all hood and fenders, with the passenger compartment better than half way back, and the boattail barely extending beyond the radius of the rear wheels.

The SSK, or Super Sport Kurz (Kurz being German for short), had a wheelbase measuring just 2,950 millimeters (approximately 116 inches), some 450 millimeters (17 3/4 inches) shorter than the SS chassis. With the limitations of a short chassis, Murphy designers concentrated the power of the body around a small, raked windscreen and cut-down doors, two distinguishing features which somehow manage in their abridged dimensions to balance a hood and cowl nearly three-quarters of the car's length. Even more remarkable is that the

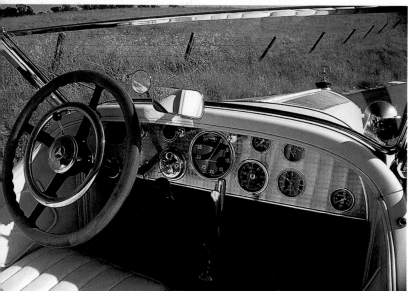

A Mercedes-Benz SSK was an impressive automobile no matter what type of body it was fitted with, but this Boattail Speedster, designed and built in the United States by the Walter M. Murphy Co. of Pasadena, California, was undoubtedly one of the most unusual ever done. One of only two SSK models bodied in this country, the other also by Murphy, the boattail design was a difficult fit on the short Mercedes chassis, since better than half of the body was consumed by the hood and cockpit.

The massive Mercedes-Benz steering wheel was the focal point of the rather close-quarter interior. Although instruments could be mounted in almost any configuration, Murphy went with an engine-turned polished brass fascia. This is the basic design that Duesenberg would use a year later on the Model J, although it was purely coincidental.

boattail, which has traditionally been the dominant characteristic in this type of design, took on a subordinate role to the rest of the body. A unique solution to designing one of the rarest SSK Mercedes ever built.

Sometimes breaking traditions was the idea behind choosing a foreign coachbuilder. In 1947, the esteemed Paris salon of Franay, where General Charles de Gaulle, England's Edward VIII, Prince Nicholas of Romania, the King of Sweden, several maharajahs, French noblemen, and a Vanderbilt or two shopped for coachwork, produced the most avant-garde Bentley of the postwar era. The car had no resemblance whatsoever to anything even remotely British;

considering it was ordered by a Frenchman, in a country known for national pride, this was just as well.

Commissioned by Monsieur E. Gadol, of Boulogne, the right-hand-drive Bentley Mk VI chassis was ordered from Franco-Britannia Motors, Ltd., in Paris, and delivered to the Franay Brothers salon on the *rue du Caporal Peugeot*, July 3, 1947.

Gadol wanted his coachbuilt cabriolet on the finest chassis available, which in 1947, was the Mk VI Bentley. In the Mk VI, Rolls-Royce had the most advanced driving platform in the company's history, a completely new chassis that had been destined for formal introduction as the Mk V in 1940. The engine of the Mk V (and Mk

Most Duesenbergs were built for people who wanted to attract attention. This car was owned by the woman famous for wanting to be alone, actress Greta Garbo. Ordered by E.Z. Sadovich of Motor Deluxe on the rue de Berri, Paris, the 1932 Model J chassis (J-481) was bodied as a Convertible Victoria by Fernandez & Darrin. Sadovich actually ordered two cars, both designed by American stylist Howard "Dutch" Darrin. The second, on chassis J-499, was for a Prince. Among the distinctive features of both cars are the elongated pontoon fenders, extremely low windshield, absence of running boards, (Darrin abhorred running boards), and the stylish pontoon-shaped step plate. On the long, 154-inch wheelbase chassis, the lines of the Darrin car seemed utterly massive, which in fact they were. This is the largest Convertible Victoria ever built.

A Proper Motor Car, or PMC; that's what the British call the Rolls-Royce. Harry C. Hatch agreed, only he preferred Packards, so the millionaire liquor distiller had a 1938 Packard Super Eight chassis delivered to Barker at 66 South Audley Street in London to be fitted with a Sedanca de Ville body like those built by Barker for the Royal Family. Certainly one of the most impressive Packards of the 1930s, Hatch's handsome livery barely had a Packard trait left except for the grille. The car is now part of the Jerry Livoni collection.

*Darrin had been designing coachwork in France since the late 1920s, and he produced several Duesenberg bodies for Sadovich over the years. Darrin preferred the Model J because the 265-horsepower Duesenberg straight-eight could handle the weight of a custom body without sacrificing performance. Even with the massive Convertible Victoria body, the Model J could reach nearly 100 miles per hour.*

*During his years in Paris, Darrin designed and built roughly ten Duesenberg bodies. This was likely the last one, built on the short 142-1/2-inch wheelbase supercharged SJ chassis (J-542) in 1935. The demand for coachbuilt cars in Europe was beginning to decline by 1935, and Darrin was thinking about returning to the United States. Some years later he said that, "The handwriting was on the wall in the custom body business by then, in fact it had just about knocked down the wall!" Like most of Darrin's Duesenberg commissions, this Convertible Victoria, now owned by Gene Cofer, was also ordered by E.Z. Sadovich, and delivered in May 1935 to Vincente Fiermonte and his wife Madeleine, the former Mrs. Jacob J. Astor.*

VI) was similar to that of the Rolls-Royce Wraith, as was the chassis, with a new independent front suspension supported by coil springs, wishbones, and an anti-roll torsion bar. The suspension geometry for the Bentley differed slightly from that of the Wraith to give the Bentley more responsive handling commensurate with its sportier image. The rear suspension on both models was a hypoid-bevel axle located by gaitered half-elliptic springs. The Mk VI was applauded as the best built, best handling car Rolls-Royce Bentley had built up to that time.

For the coachwork on the Bentley, the Franays had the luxury of capitalizing on two decades of French styling, not only their own, but of Figoni and Saoutchik as well. The finished car was shown on the Franay stand at the Paris Salon de l'Auto among a gathering of stunning works from Figoni, Saoutchik, and Chapron. The Bentley Cabriolet, however, was absolutely overwhelming, with grand, sweeping, fully enclosed fenders, rakish body lines and curves, and bold chrome embellishments.

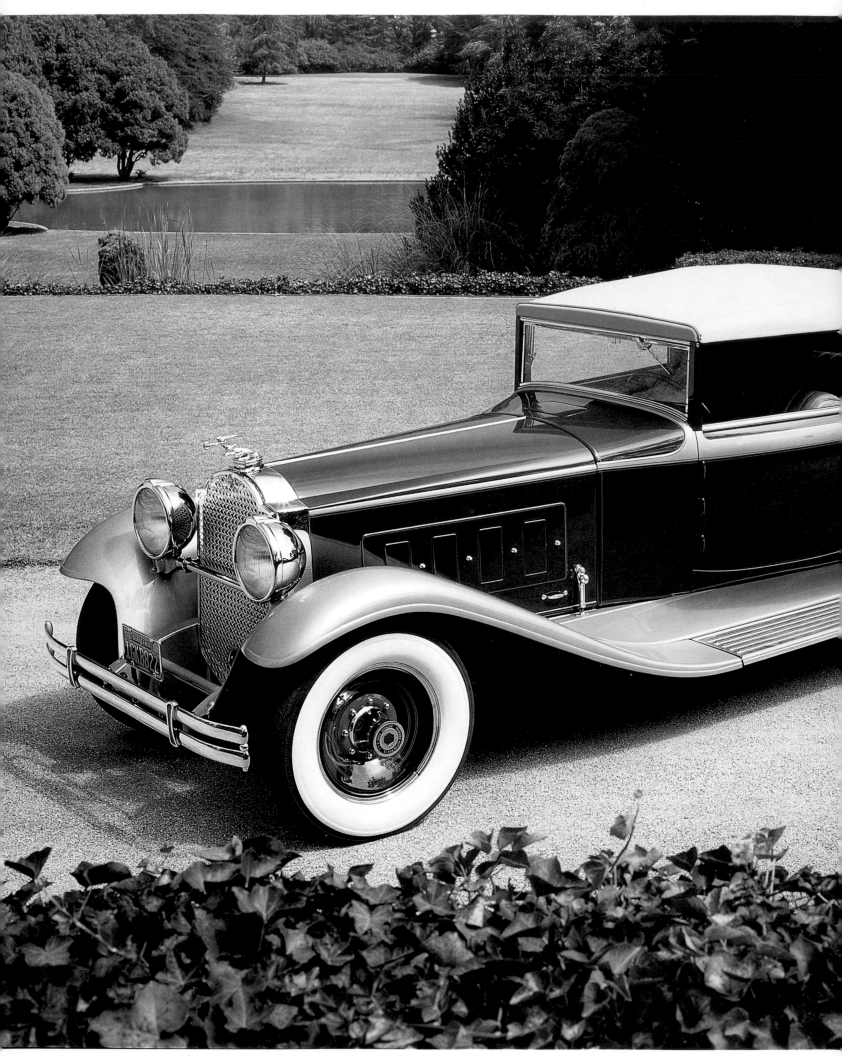

*Packards were among the most popular American makes in France. Franay bodied several in the 1930s, and carrossier Maurice Proux of Paris designed and built this aristocratic two-door Victoria on a 1930 Packard 745 chassis. Along with an L-29 Cord, this is believed to be the only other American car bodied by the Courbevoie-Paris carrossier. The entire body is steel, and Proux discarded all of the standard factory equipment, building his own fenders, hood, and cowl. Proux's fender styling is distinguished by the tapered bead, which begins at the inside front curve and trails along the outer edge, with the reveal progressively getting thinner until it disappears at the start of the running board and picks up again at the base of the rear fender. Another unusual Proux characteristic is the door design, which curves down at the bottom, rather than being straight across.*

It has become one of the most alluring cars of the postwar 1940s, nationality notwithstanding.

The Bentley was so well received that in 1948, it won the Grand Prix in all categories at the Enghien Concours d' Elegance and the Premier Prix award at the Bois de Boulogne Concours, shows traditionally known for favoring French cars. After winning two of the highest awards in France, Gadol simply drove and enjoyed his Bentley for the next several years, finally selling it to an admirer in 1951.

There are a hundred such stories throughout classic car history, tales of great cars fitted with hand-built custom bodies conceived of and fashioned in a country other than the chassis maker's. Each was a unique design, combining talents, technologies, and parts from two continents, very much what is done today in the construction of virtually every American, European, and Japanese car built. In the 1990s, this melding of technologies is what we call a world car. In the 1930s, *worldly car* would have been more appropriate.

# Chapter Seven

# Limousines, Town Cars, and Broughams

## The Most Beautiful Formal Cars Ever Built

For more than two centuries limousines, whether horse-drawn or horse-powered, have possessed a certain mystique, as far back as eighteenth-century carriages built for European nobility. The hoi polloi always knew that coddled within was someone of consequence—a duke, a prime minister, perhaps a land baron, or the mistress of one of the aforementioned.

America's foremost carriage maker was Brewster, founded by James Brewster, a descendant of Elder William Brewster, who came to Plymouth Colony on the *Mayflower* in 1620. Brewster opened his first carriage-building factory in New Haven, Connecticut, in 1810. His innovative designs introduced many advanced manufacturing techniques, which helped establish the firm as one of the country's leading carriage makers and New Haven as the coachbuilding hub of America in the 1800s.

Among collectors of horse-drawn carriages, a Brewster is the Rolls-Royce of its time, and perhaps even that is an understatement, according to noted carriage and car collector Gene Epstein.

"Brewster was known world wide, not only for the artistry of their carriages but the craftsmanship and ingenuity that went into making each a work of art. Only those fortunate enough to be in a high-income position could afford a Brewster carriage," says Epstein, who owns 12 vintage models dating from 1895 to 1909. "Throughout the 1800s Brewster remained in

*A formal car in the British tradition, this 1938 Packard Model 1605 Super Eight was bodied in England by Barker with coachwork based on Rolls-Royce styling frequently used by Barker for members of the Royal Family. The Packard is now owned by Jerry Livoni.*

*The only example ever produced in this style on a Packard chassis, the Barker body was all aluminum. However, with a built-in bar, twin vanities, a built-in safe, and power divider window, the overall weight of the car was in excess of 5,000 pounds.*

the forefront of carriage makers the world over. He had a compassion and a passion to build the finest carriages. His company produced the highest quality coaches that anyone had ever seen."

In 1827, a branch factory was opened in Bridgeport and another at 52 Broad Street in New York City. They were managed by Brewster's two sons, James and Henry, until the 1840s when they left to form their own companies. In 1848, there were three Brewster coachworks in New York: James Brewster & Sons, James B. Brewster Co., and Henry Brewster Co.

Henry and partners James W. Lawrence and John W. Britton opened a new factory at 372-4 Broome Street in 1856. In the 1860s, James renamed his firm Brewster & Baldwin as successor to the original James Brewster & Sons. Henry also changed the name of his company to Messrs. Brewster & Co. of Broome St. He continued to use the name even when the establishment moved into a new five-story building at 1581 Broadway.

It was Henry's company that eventually lent the Brewster name to the automotive coachbuilding trade in 1905. Joining several other noted American carriage makers, such as A.T. Demarest & Co. of New York, the Derham Body Co. in Rosemont, Pennsylvania, and Brunn & Co. in Buffalo, New York, Brewster & Co. began designing and manufacturing coachbuilt bodies for a variety of American and imported chassis, particularly Rolls-Royce.

Realizing the potential of the automobile business, Henry's son William moved operations into a new 420,000-square foot factory at 27-01 Bridge Plaza North, across the East River from Manhattan in Long Island City, Queens, and in 1914, became the sales agent for Rolls-Royce, Ltd. Brewster & Co. remained the principal coachbuilder for Rolls-Royce in the United States through late 1916, when chassis shipments were curtailed due to World War I.

In addition to custom coachwork, Brewster manufactured its own line of automobiles, powered by four-cylinder Knight-type engines, from around 1915 to 1925, the year in which Rolls-Royce of America, Inc., purchased Brewster. Rolls-Royce of America, however, became one of the Depression's many automotive casualties, going into receivership in 1934. John S. Inskip, who had headed RROA and Brewster since 1925, came up with the idea of fitting coachbuilt bodies on modified Ford V-8 chassis as a way of keeping the Brewster operation solvent. Combining the luxury of bespoke coachwork with the economical price of a Ford chassis, the cars had a selling price of only $3,500. While that was nearly six times what Ford's top-of-the-line models sold for, it was half what one expected to pay for a custom-built body in the 1930s. Brewster offered a total of four styles on the lengthened 127-inch Ford chassis: town car, limousine, convertible coupe, and convertible sedan, all carrying the same price tag.

*One of the most luxurious Mercedes-Benz town cars built in the 1920s was bodied in Italy by carrozzeria Castagna for Tulsa, Oklahoma, oilman Charles Murray and his wife Marion Downs, the great-granddaughter of Churchill Downs. The car cost Murray an astounding $28,000 in 1927 and took the better part of 1927 to build. The Murrays spent little time in Tulsa; they lived in the penthouse of the Waldorf-Astoria in New York. Mrs. Murray hired a German chauffeur to drive the town car during the five years the family resided in New York. She recalled some 40 years later that even in the 1930s when there were many custom-built town cars in New York, the Mercedes-Benz still caused quite a stir when it was driven through downtown. The carved mahogany trim and luxurious brocaded silk upholstery created by Castagna for the Mercedes was one of the most elaborate interiors ever done by the Milan coachbuilder. The interior was later redone in beige broadcloth, as it is today. The car is now part of the Blackhawk collection*

---

A 1930s-era Brewster limousine could be built on any chassis the customer requested. But regardless of make, each was unmistakably a Brewster design, characterized by the sweeping, heart-shaped grille that became the company's trademark. Brewster was the only American coachbuilder to establish a styling cue so powerful that it became more important than either the chassis or body style of the automobile. Whether it was a Ford, Lincoln, Buick, or Cadillac limousine became of secondary importance to the fact that it was first a Brewster. The cars became so popular, that in 1934, Cole Porter used a Brewster as one of many praiseworthy objects in the song "You're the Top" from the Broadway musical *Anything Goes*. "You're the top, you're a Brewster body..." Porter himself was a Brewster owner, along with Al Jolson, Fred Waring, Edsel Ford, and even Vincent Astor.

The stylish coachwork, distinguished by the captivating grille shell, split front bumpers, and flared front fenders, was designed by J.S. Inskip, who also penned the exquisite Ascot and Derby Rolls-Royce bodies.

Brewster Fords and Brewster bodies were produced through 1942 in a section of the Long Island City factory, which reverted back to the Brewster family in 1936. While it is estimated that some 300 cars left the Brewster factory, only those with the grille, bumper, and fender treatments can be classified as true Brewsters.

In 1940, the firm built a stunning town car on a Buick Series 90 chassis for Mr. Jay Whitney, former president of the New York Stock Exchange. The Brewster was kept at the Whitney's Vermont summer home and after the war was given to the family chauffeur.

The Buick remained in the chauffeur's care until 1962, when he advertised the car for sale in the *New York Times*. It was purchased by collector Noel Thompson. Recalls Noel, "I wanted the town car so that my wife Jean and I could sit up front and put our four kids in the enclosed rear compartment! The Brewster body was specially designed to fit the Buick's 140-inch wheelbase chassis, and it did not have the typical Brewster-style flared fenders. Instead they were rolled over. From what I understand, Mr. Whitney paid $18,000 to have the car built."

The rear passenger compartment of the town car was luxuriously upholstered in tan broadcloth, and the large bench seat was stuffed with goose down for added comfort. There were also two fold-out jump seats in the rear. The driver's compartment was finished in black leather. "One unusual feature," says Thompson, "is that Brewster used P100 headlights on this car, which were used on early Rolls-Royce models. The car also had a chromed bronze reproduction of Lalique's *Spirit of the Wind* hood ornament when I purchased it."

The Series 90 chassis was available for custom coachwork in 1940 as part of Buick President Harlow Curtice's image-building program. His division was hot on the heels of Cadillac, and Curtice wanted to move one step closer to GM's top luxury marque.

Total Buick sales reached 283,404 in 1940; Buick's best model year ever to that time. Although Harlow Curtice had given the go-ahead for cataloged customs, the coachbuilt Buicks, designed and built by Brunn & Co. of Buffalo, did not appear until the 1941 model year. By then, Cadillac complained so vehemently to GM

*Cadillac was one of the first automakers in the world to introduce a limousine. From 1914 on, luxurious enclosed cars were a Cadillac hallmark. The original design never waned in popularity, remaining not only fashionable well into the 1940s, but the most expensive model offered by Cadillac. This handsome 1937 Fleetwood Formal Sedan, now in the Herb Rothman/Ted Davidson collection, is typical of the company's superb coachwork and luxurious interior design. Cadillac was one of the first manufacturers to introduce the solid steel turret-top design, a solid roof structure covered from the front to the rear quarters in genuine English leather. The choice of fabrics for the interior characterized Fleetwood's claim of building cars with "faultless good taste." Fabric choices for Cadillac limousines, formal sedans, and town cars were bedford cord, vogue weave broadcloth, and textured cloth in either tan, brown, or gray.*

management about direct competition within the divisions that Curtice was directed to abandon his plans to offer Brunn bodies.

As for pure customs, Buick continued to offer chassis as it had in the past, and anyone could have a custom Buick made to order by an independent coachbuilder. However, by 1940 the demand was practically nil, and the Brewster Series 90 Buick town car was one of the few ever built.

The design of a limousine or town car was often a very personal matter. The specific needs or demands of an owner often dictated the designer's rendition. Such was the Murphy-bodied Buick town car created for Charles and Anita Howard back in 1931.

Charles Howard was the Buick distributor for the western United States, so driving anything but a Buick would have been inappropriate. Of course, there was nothing to prevent Howard from having a Duesenberg-style body built by Murphy to fit the Buick chassis.

In 1932, Buick offered four model ranges: the Series 50, Series 60, Series 80, and Series 90. There were a total of eight standard body styles for the Series 50, seven for the Series 60, two for the Series 80, and nine for the Series 90. Within the Series 90, a total of 24 chassis were delivered for full custom coachwork, including one sent to Murphy by Charles Howard, upon which he had the town car body refitted, so that it would be on the latest Buick chassis.

Examples such as the Murphy and Brewster Buick town cars represent the epitome of an era when luxury was a very individualistic consideration, and coachwork could be tailored to an owner like a bespoke suit.

For Cadillac, America's preeminent builder of luxury cars, the chauffeur-driven limousine has been associated with the name since 1906 when the company introduced its first seven-passenger model, a design not far removed in character from Brewster's great formal horse-drawn carriages of the late nineteenth century.

The basic concept of a tall, luxuriously appointed aft cabin, separated by a divider window from the driver's forward outdoor

compartment, changed little until 1914, when Cadillac introduced its first fully enclosed limousine. The original open design—also known as a Formal Town Car and Limousine Brougham—never waned in popularity, remaining not only fashionable well into the 1940s, but the most expensive model offered by Cadillac.

Although Cadillac owned the prestige name in limousines and town cars throughout the 1920s and 1930s, Lincolns were generally the most attractively styled of the two marques. This was due for the most part to Edsel Ford, whose exceptional sense of style had guided the company's selection of coachwork and coachbuilders since the Ford Motor Company purchased Lincoln from the Lelands in 1922.

Edsel was a stylist at heart, and when a particular custom body appealed to his aesthetic tastes, he would contract for its production on a semi-custom basis. As a result, Lincoln customers had access to body designs that would otherwise have been limited to, and priced as, full customs.

Edsel's talent for styling was matched only by his ability to befriend some of the top automotive designers in the country, giving Lincoln access to the latest creations from Dietrich, Locke, Brunn, and Derham, among others. Thanks to Edsel Ford, Lincoln had one of the finest selections of coachwork available on any American luxury car sold in the 1920s and early 1930s.

He was also an aggressive marketer. In 1927, Edsel selected a spectacular Club Roadster, designed by his friend Ray Dietrich, to represent the Lincoln Motorcar Company at the Paris Concours d'Elegance. To everyone's surprise, with the possible exception of Edsel Ford himself, the Dietrich Club Roadster won the Gold Medal for Design. From Paris, the car was sent to Milan, Italy, where it won again, competing against 72 other designs. The Lincoln concluded its rout of Europe in Monte Carlo, where it again took top honors for design plus the Grand Prix as the best car overall.

Ford sent an entire series of Lincolns on tour across Europe in 1927, each bearing a specific period theme represented in the

*A car with more mileage in the hold of a steamship than on the highways of the world, this 1930 Model J Duesenberg was built for newspaper publisher William Randolph Hearst by Americans Dutch Darrin and Tom Hibbard at their carrossier in Paris, France. The chassis was shipped to France, then returned to New York, and transported to California, where Hearst gave the Hibbard & Darrin Transformable Cabriolet to actress Marion Davies. The car spent most of its life at La Cuesta Encantada, Hearst's castle in San Simeon, California. In a book written by Marion Davies, the car was shown in pictures taken all over the world. Whenever she traveled with Hearst, they had the Duesenberg shipped on ahead so it would be waiting for them when they arrived. The Hibbard & Darrin design featured a three-position top that could allow the car to be driven fully enclosed, with an open chauffeur's compartment (as pictured), or with the entire top lowered. The car is currently owned by Jerry J. Moore.*

styling of the coachwork, trim, and paint schemes. Edsel considered this the consummation of refined motorcar magnificence. Among the periods displayed were Louis XIV, on a Locke-bodied French Brougham; the Renaissance, captured with a Brunn Cabriolet; Gothic, portrayed as a Limousine by Willoughby; Roman, depicted by Dietrich with a stylish Convertible; Egyptian, defined by Judkins with a Two-Window Berline; Oriental, rendered by Ralph Robert's LeBaron Four-Passenger Coupe; Georgian, on a Limousine bodied by Locke; a Dietrich Sport Phaeton was chosen to define Modern; Colonial was rendered by Willoughby with a genteel Cabriolet; and French Empire by Holbrook, which built a regal Cabriolet Sedan.

This stunning array of Lincoln customs captivated Europe's café society, resulting in a number of foreign orders in 1927, including one taken by Fleetwood from a client in France for a massive seven-passenger Victoria town car, one of the last bodies produced by Fleetwood on anything but a Cadillac chassis. By 1927, Fleetwood was working almost exclusively for GM, and by year's end the Pennsylvania coachbuilder had become a subsidiary of General Motors.

For the better part of the automobile's history in America, Fleetwood had been designing custom coachwork, and the firm was no stranger to foreign orders having become well known in the 1920s for its work on Maybach, Lancia, Fiat, Renault, Minerva,

*The most famous Packard of the 1930s, the Dietrich Style 3182 Special Sport Sedan was built on the 147-inch wheelbase 1107 chassis and exhibited as the centerpiece of the Travel and Transportation Building exhibit at the 1933 Century of Progress World's Fair in Chicago. The Dietrich Packard was honored by being selected to represent the epitome of motor car transportation for 1933. Nearly 65 years after it was built, the car is still in almost all-original condition, including the highly polished burled Carpathian elm interior trim. The car is now part of the Otis Chandler collection.*

---

and Benz chassis, among others. In 1926, Fleetwood built the stunning Isotta-Fraschini roadster for film star Rudolph Valentino, and it was Fleetwood's international renown among the rich and famous that led to the coachbuilder being chosen to design and manufacture the largest Victoria ever built on a Lincoln chassis.

As ordered, specifications for the Victoria included a separate driver's compartment, dual rear seating area, and dual rear windshields. For such a car, Fleetwood needed a longer wheelbase than the standard 136-inch Lincoln platform. A 150-inch Commercial Chassis, usually supplied to professional car builders for the installation of hearse and ambulance bodies, was used, and even that wasn't enough. The expansive length of car was extended further by fitting two luggage trunks in tandem, adding another 3 feet beyond the rear bumper of the massive Lincoln.

The owner had requested a body style that would be perceived as formal and elegant, like a great royal coach. Thus by 1927 stan-

dards, the styling of the Fleetwood Imperial Victoria was dated, resembling the Park Phaetons fashionable on Locomobile and Peerless chassis of the 1906-1910 period. The Lincoln Imperial Victoria was a visually imposing automobile, 10 inches longer, 6 inches higher, and 2 inches wider than the average formal Lincoln of 1927. The massive 12 1/2-foot span between the wheels was consumed by four large doors with ornate carriage-type handles, a set of arm-chair jump seats, a large rear seat, and two folding windshields. With an appearance that was decidedly French in flavor, the Lincoln Victoria with its American-made body became the toast of Paris in 1927.

*There is perhaps no greater example from the 1930s than this Buick Series 90 to demonstrate the fact that coachwork made the car. It was custom-bodied by the Walter M. Murphy Co. in Pasadena, California, to resemble a Duesenberg. Murphy's typical Duesenberg styling is evident in the rakishly angled windshield, most atypical of town car styling, except for a Duesenberg. The body is lower and narrower, with sportier, less formal lines, also typical of Murphy Duesenbergs. And what appears to be chrome trim on the upper half of the car is actually the polished aluminum body itself. The only remaining traces of Buick styling are the grille shell, the side panels of the hood (Murphy built the top of the hood), and the bumpers. At the rear, a Model J-style trunk rack was added above a solid mahogany deck replacing the Buick rear splash pan. The car was designed for Anita Howard, wife of the Buick distributor for the Western United States. Her monogram can be seen in front of the grille guard and in the polished aluminum trim on the rear doors.*

---

Packard produced as many formal cars as Cadillac and Lincoln in the 1920s and 1930s. To show how important closed cars were to the Packard image, a Dietrich-designed limousine, known as a Special Sport Sedan, was chosen by Packard to represent the company at the 1933 Century of Progress World's Fair in Chicago. Built along the waterfront of Lake Michigan, the Chicago Exposition's architecture was a brilliant montage of color and form, the latest in art deco, modern, and contemporary designs, and as the Fair's centerpiece, the giant dome of the Travel and Transportation Building rose a majestic 12 stories above the fairgrounds. It was there, under the dome, that an art jury was asked to designate one automobile to represent the epitome of motorcar transportation for 1933. They did not choose a sporty phaeton or speedster; they selected the elegant Dietrich Packard.

Later known as the "Car of the Dome," the 1933 Packard was Dietrich Style 3182, built on an 1107 chassis. Dietrich's design, actually penned in 1930, before he left Packard to work for Chrysler, featured a low roofline, V windshield, and sweeping fenders, accentuated by stylist Alexis de Sakhnoffsky's famed "false hood," which gave the car the appearance of added length by eliminating the cowl and taking the hood line all the way back to the windshield. The car was not only selected for its exterior styling, but for its interior design and appointments, described by Packard in 1933:

*Aside from its unique lines, this Packard is of special interest because of the costliness of its interior furnishings. All body hardware is heavily gold plated and so are the steering column and instruments. Wood paneling and trim are highly polished burled Carpathian elm. Built into the back of the front seat is a cabinet extending the full width of the car. The right side is occupied by a full length dressing case with gold plated fittings. At the left is a cellarette with a drop door which becomes a glass covered table when lowered. Upholstery is especially selected beige broadcloth. The exterior finish is called Sun Glow Pearl, a new finish which is gold, brown, or pearl, depending upon how the light strikes it.*

Built on the 147-inch wheelbase chassis, the "Car of the Dome" was updated in August 1933 to reflect new fender, bumper, and cowl vent styling for the model year, which began three months after the Exposition opened. A Packard crew came in and made the changes overnight, so the next morning the car had all of the new 1933 features.

*In the November 16, 1936 issue of* Time *magazine, this Model SJ Duesenberg Town Car, bodied by Bohman & Schwartz, was noted as being "The most expensive car in the United States." Designed by Auburn, Cord, Duesenberg stylist J. Herbert Newport for actress Mae West, the car was ultimately purchased by Ethel V. Mars, of the Mars Candy Company, for a reported $20,000. Aside from the renowned Twenty Grand Duesenberg built for the 1933 Chicago World's Fair, and so named for its price, this was the most expensive Model SJ built in the United States. Newport and Bohman & Schwartz created a truly unique design that was never duplicated.*

In an historical sense, this was perhaps the most important car in Packard's history. At the time of the Chicago World's Fair, the automobile as a concept and recognized mode of personal transportation was only 47 years old. Among all of the cars available in 1933, Duesenberg, Cadillac, Mercedes-Benz, Lincoln, Marmon, Hispano-Suiza, Pierce-Arrow, to name but a few, this was the one chosen to represent the automobile in its grandest form.

Among a handful of exceptional town cars assembled on the Duesenberg Model J and SJ chassis was one designed by stylist Herb Newport for actress Mae West, and built in 1935 by Pasadena coachbuilder Bohman & Schwartz.

Herb Newport, Christian Bohman, and Maurice Schwartz favored streamlined coachwork—fluid, rolling forms devoid of any hard lines. For Bohman & Schwartz, even the traditional upright

Duesenberg grille was not sacred. Bohman had left Murphy in 1930, and Schwartz in 1932, when Walter M. Murphy closed the doors to his renowned shop. In April, Bohman and Schwartz formed their own company and hired most of the ex-Murphy staff. The scope of their business ranged from minor body modifications to complete frame-up designs, many for Hollywood celebrities and for use in movies, such as the wildly styled Buick featured in the 1936 film *Topper*.

Bohman & Schwartz built nine Duesenberg bodies and redesigned several, including a Rollston JN Convertible for Clark Gable and a Murphy Convertible Coupe for Mae West. Unfortunately, when the 1935 Newport-designed town car was completed, the actress didn't care for the streamlined body and camel hump spare tire mounts. Wealthy socialite Ethel Mars, of the Mars Candy

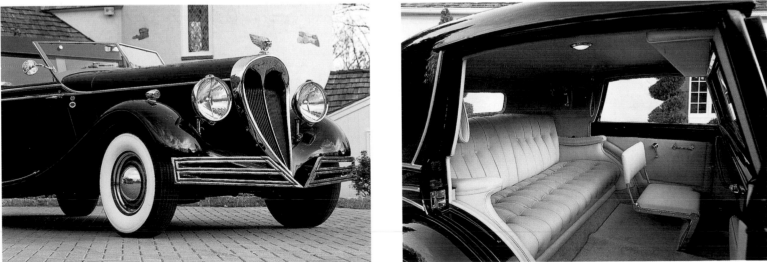

It is interesting that two of the most unusual custom-bodied town cars of the classic era were both built on Buick Series 90 chassis. In 1940, Brewster built this stunning town car for Mr. Jay Whitney, former president of the New York Stock Exchange. The Brewster's stylish coachwork is distinguished by the heart-shaped grille shell and split front bumpers. The driver's compartment was upholstered in black leather, while the handsome rear compartment with divider window was upholstered in tan broadcloth. The rear seat was stuffed with goose down, and there were also two fold-out jump seats. The car is now owned by Noel Thompson.

*There was a time—an elegant, wonderful time—when going out was an event. And when the master or mistress of the house asked to have the car brought around, both a chauffeur and a valet were required to prepare the vehicle. The chauffeur was also the occasional mechanic, whose duties necessitated an exhaustive knowledge of the vehicle and its maintenance. For the driver of this 1927 Fleetwood-bodied Lincoln Imperial Victoria, built for a client in Paris, France, the chauffeur had it pretty good, because Lincoln was one of the most reliable automobiles of its time. Powered by a 357.8-cubic inch V-8, the 90-horsepower output was sufficient to propel even a car of this size to 85 miles per hour. Fleetwood equipped the Victoria, which cost $15,000 to build, with dual spot lamps and headlights, by Marchal of France, and a pair of German silver electric carriage lamps. This Lincoln is now in the Jack Dunning collection.*

---

Company, saw the car and thought that the sleek Duesenberg was absolutely stunning, purchasing it from Bohman & Schwartz on April 14, 1935.

Among all the Duesenbergs bodied in America, this is perhaps the most sublime, quite an achievement considering the number of designs by Gordon Buehrig, Frank Hershey, and Ray Dietrich, which were done for Duesenberg. In the November 16, 1936, issue of *Time* magazine, the Ethel Mars town car was noted as "The most expensive car in the United States." Mars paid Bohman & Schwartz a record $20,000 for the supercharged Model J.

It seems that architects and industrial designers have been dabbling with automotive design for a long time. Raymond Loewy penned a number of cars, including the Studebaker Avanti; Norman Bel Geddes did the Graham, restyled Airflow, and Nashes; and Wal-

*By 1942, automotive styling had changed drastically. A year before, Cadillac had thrown everyone for a loop with the most beautiful and stylish Sixty Special ever built, and sleek fastback styling for the Series 61 and 62 lines, but boxier styling for the Fleetwood Series 75 Formal Sedans and Limousines. By 1942, formal cars like this Model 67 Limousine were sporting the conservative styling that would reappear on Cadillac's Fleetwood 75 Sedans and Limousines in 1946. Bear in mind, that for the period, they were received as the latest and most modern cars offered by Cadillac in more than a decade. Yet, if you look back at models like the 1937 Fleetwood Formal Sedan, the graceful elegance and classic body lines of the late 1930s were somehow lost in the design of American cars built in the 1940s. Chalk it up to progress.*

The

Brunn-bodied Lincoln Touring Cabriolet was introduced in 1936 as a combination open and closed car. The unique design by Hermann Brunn provided for a convertible rear quarter, allowing the passengers to enjoy open-air driving. The chauffeur, separated from the rear by a glass divider window, was enclosed in a hardtop with two tinted skylights above the windshield header. The design was included by Edsel Ford in the 1937 Lincoln model line. The Brunn design was also offered on Packard models in 1938. The Lincoln version sold for $8,000, the Packard for $10,000.

*In 1946, automotive stylist Raymond Loewy decided to produce two Lincoln Continental limousines for his personal use. Starting with a pair of used 1941 coupes, the Continentals were dropped 6 inches over their frames, the fenderlines, grilles, and deck lids modified to Loewy's specifications, and the cars were fitted with Coupé de Ville-style roofs featuring a removable plexiglass cover for the chauffeur's compartment.*

---

ter Dorwin Teague did a Marmon. Architects like Buckminster Fuller, Walter Gropius, and Frank Lloyd Wright also took their turn at drafting automobiles. Shortly after taking delivery of a 1940 Lincoln Continental Cabriolet, Frank Lloyd Wright's daughter had an accident with the car and he saw this as an opportunity to add some design features of his own while it was being repaired.

Wright had the Continental body lowered, cut the windshield down by some 5 inches, dropped the rear seating height, and constructed a Coupé de Ville roof. The new half-roof had two semi-circular opera windows that could be opened out, and absolutely no rear window at all! The front seat was upholstered in leather while the entire rear compartment, including headliner, was done in gray wool. Wright had the car painted Taliesin red—a bright orange-tinged brick red hue that was his trademark color. This was the only car he ever designed.

Raymond Loewy was once described by *Time* magazine as the leader of the industrial design profession. To his credit were designs

*Architect Frank Lloyd Wright had a 1940 Continental body customized as his personal limousine. The Lincoln windshield was cut down by some 5 inches, the rear seating height dropped, and the roof rebuilt into a Coupé de Ville design. The unusual car had two small half-moon opera windows and no backlight. This no doubt made putting the car in reverse quite a challenge for the driver!*

for more than 50 of *Fortune* magazine's top 500 companies, and many of his designs, ranging from refrigerators and streamliner trains to the Coca Cola bottle, have literally become American icons. In addition to designing cars for Studebaker, which included the first postwar models, the 1953 Starliner Coupe, and 1962 Avanti, Loewy had numerous automobiles modified to his own specifications, including a pair of used 1941 Lincoln Continentals purchased in 1946.

Loewy's intent was to design a chauffeur-driven Continental limousine. The cars were sent along with his styling recommendations to the Durham coachworks in Rosemont, Pennsylvania, where the tops were completely severed and the cars stripped of all body trim. The Continentals were then dropped 6 inches over their frames, which were modified to support the extra weight of the custom bodies. New roofs were fitted with a half enclosure for the rear and a removable plexiglass cover over the chauffeur's compartment. Recessed into the roof was a hinged glass partition with folding wind wings that could be lowered and latched to the front

seatback. In a matter of moments, the Continental could be transformed into a dual windshield town car.

Loewy's design, on one car, did away with the 1941 grille, bumpers, and traditional rear-mounted spare and incorporated a Studebaker grille and bumper for the front, and reshaped fenders. The interiors were completely customized, with the front upholstered in beige broadcloth with beige synthetic pigskin trim, and the rear compartment in a soft, lettuce-green broadcloth. Of the two cars built by Derham, one was kept stateside and the other shipped to Loewy's Paris, France, home. Today, they are both in private collections.

Among American and European Classics, phaetons and roadsters are the most valuable today, but in their time, these cars were far less expensive than limousines, town cars, and broughams. In fact, with very few exceptions, the most expensive models of the 1920s and 1930s were the luxurious closed cars of the aristocracy.

# Chapter Eight

# Postwar Classics— American and European Cars 1945 to 1948

## *The End of an Era*

W hen World War II came to an end in 1945, the automobile industry was one of the first to gear up for peacetime manufacturing. However, in Europe, unlike the United States, the war had extended right up to the front doors of the world's leading auto makers. Daimler-Benz was in near ruin with its factories in Stuttgart, Mannheim, Untertürkheim, Gaggenau, and Sindelfingen practically leveled to their foundations by Allied bombing raids. There wouldn't be another automobile with a silver star atop its grille until 1947, and at that, only a simple 170 Sedan with either a four-cylinder gas or diesel engine. It was about the only car for which tooling remained intact. Mercedes-Benz would not introduce a new luxury or sports model until 1951.

BMW, which had been one of Germany's leading auto makers throughout the late 1930s, was a divided and broken company by 1946, with its management in West Germany and all of its primary manufacturing facilities at Eisenach under Soviet control in the East. BMW would not produce another car until 1952. The Auto Union was all but finished, with most of its factories in the Soviet sector, and Maybach was unable to resume automobile production. So as far as new cars were concerned, Germany was out of the early postwar picture.

---

*The Alfa Romeo 6C 2500 was among the first sports cars to come from Italy after World War II. The superbly styled coachwork by Pininfarina for the Cabriolets was supplied for both the 118-inch wheelbase Sport models (this page, from the Jerry McAlevy collection) and 118-inch wheelbase Super Sport models (following page). The red Super Sport was owned by actor Tyrone Power and featured in the film* The Barefoot Contessa.

Among the first European auto makers to get back into production was Alfa Romeo, with the 6C 2500 models originally built from 1939 through 1941. Because the cars spanned both prewar and postwar periods, it is difficult to categorize their sleek, envelope-style body design as indicative of either era. It is definitely not vintage in the sense of a "1930s" Alfa Romeo, yet it is far from being a contemporary postwar car. With Solomon-like wisdom, prewar models are granted Classic status by the CCCA and postwar cars are recognized by the Milestone Car Society. For Alfa Romeo a double *fait accompli*.

The 6C 2500 has become one of the most desirable of Alfa Romeo models, in either prewar or postwar versions, and is among the last coachbuilt production sports cars to be manufactured in Italy. The 6C 2500 Sport and Super Sport chassis were fitted with cabriolet bodies by Pininfarina, and with closed coachwork by Touring. The Pininfarina cabriolets were characterized by simple, uncomplicated lines, and a low, wide stance not too different from the Pininfarina-designed Cisitalia. The bumpers were almost nonexistent, leaving the tall Alfa grille unchallenged for visual impact. The Touring coupes had similar styling cues, although slightly more flamboyant lines.

Inside either, one would find lavish appointments of rich, hand-sewn leather upholstery, plush carpeting, and a remarkable instrument panel fitted with ornate, jewel-like gauges flanked by stylish Ivorlite control knobs resembling carved ivory. The 6C 2500s were almost all designed to seat five, with three across in front and two in the narrower rear. The divided front consisted of a small, adjustable driver's seat and a wide twin passenger seat.

*Equipped with a four-wheel fully independent suspension, four-wheel hydraulic brakes, and Rudge-type wheels mounting Pirelli 6.00 x 18 tires, the Alfa Romeo 6C 2500 Sport and Super Sport models used a race-proven 2,443-cubic centimeter six-cylinder DOHC engine with hemispheric combustion chambers. Sport models had a single two-barrel carburetor, 7:1 compression ratio, and developed 90 horsepower. The higher-performance Super Sport engine (pictured) produced 105 horsepower utilizing three horizontal single-barrel carburetors and a compression of 7.5:1.*

*Inside the Alfa Romeo 6C 2500, one would find lavish appointments of rich, hand-sewn leather upholstery, plush carpeting, and a remarkable instrument panel fitted with ornate, jewel-like gauges flanked by stylish Ivorlite control knobs, resembling carved ivory. Unique to these models was a column-mounted four-speed shifter necessitated by the car's three-across front seating.*

Unusual, but far better than a traditional bench. A peculiarity of these cars was a four-speed synchromesh transmission that was integrated with the engine block, providing gear selection via a shifter mounted on the steering column. According to Alfa Romeo, this was done to accommodate the three-across front seating.

Although never intended for competition, the 6C 2500s did quite well in private hands throughout the late 1940s and early 1950s, reaffirming Alfa's guiding principle that its race cars should be suitable for the road, and its road cars suitable for racing. A pair of 6C 2500 Sport models earned a place in motorsports history, finishing fourth and eighth overall in the first Carrera PanAmericana de Mexico in 1950. Not bad for a five-passenger production car.

A total of only 2,594 6C 2500s were built from 1939 to 1953. Of that number, only 1,140 were Super Sports and 458 were Sports, the latter being discontinued in 1951.

One of the first, if not *the* first, postwar Classics to be com-

pleted in France was a 1946 Delahaye 135M Cabriolet Narval designed for the Aga Khan by Figoni et Falaschi.

Bodied as a two-seater, which was usually the competition formula (most Delahayes were designed to seat four or five), the Cabriolet Narval was the most flamboyant of Joseph Figoni's designs for the Delahaye chassis. The Aga Khan's car was hand-fabricated out of aluminum, while subsequent examples, estimated to be around five or six in number, were manufactured with steel bodies.

Among the features which set the first car apart from those that followed were a less prominent narval or "shark nose" and more gracefully sculpted front fenders. On later postwar versions, these styling cues tended to appear a bit heavy-handed.

As with nearly all Delahayes, the coachwork was intended to portray a sense of motion. In some respects, it was almost a caricature of an automobile at speed, with swept-back lines accentuated with just a trace of windshield frame, small ovoid doors, and enor-

*It is written that beauty is in the eye of the beholder. When the subject is French sports cars and French design, no statement could be more true, nor more heatedly debated. In this instance, the beauty was this 1946 Delahaye, and it was actress Rita Hayworth, whose lovely eye told her that this car was no beauty. "It looks like an aircraft carrier," she said to her beloved Prince Ali Khan, who had given her the Figoni-bodied Cabriolet Narval, originally made for his father in 1946, as a wedding gift in 1949. They subsequently divorced in 1953, presumably not as a result of her dislike for the car.*

mous elliptical fully skirted fenders. Figoni believed that enclosed wheels would produce less wind drag and, in theory, he was correct.

From the driver's seat, the view was one of enormous hood and fenders stretching what seemed to be half a car length ahead. Contrasting a seemingly outrageous exterior, the right-hand-drive Cabriolet was rather simply appointed, especially for the postwar 1940s, when clear plastics and chrome trim were becoming very popular in European design. From behind the wheel, the driver faced two large multiple gauges housed in a one-piece curved aluminum dashboard, accented with chrome speed lines running through the instruments. Figoni chose a white steering wheel with

matching Cotal pre-select shift box, mounted on the left-hand side of the column, to complete the car's sublime interior appointments.

The chassis and engine of the 135M were a development of the prewar Delahaye introduced at the Paris Auto Salon in 1933. Delahaye unveiled the new Superluxe model with a 120-horsepower 3.2-liter six-cylinder engine, front independent suspension, and large self-adjusting brakes. By design, it was a car capable of being bodied either for touring, or fitted with lightweight coachwork suited to competition.

In 1934, the Superluxe was relaunched as the Type 135, equipped with a slightly larger 3.5-liter engine. Meanwhile, the 3.2-

liter prototype of 1933, fitted with a lightweight competition body built by Figoni, was sent to the Montlhéry track where it set an endurance record averaging 117 kilometers per hour (72 miles per hour) for over 4,000 miles. This event would mark the beginning of a five-year-long motorsports campaign that would culminate in a stunning first, second, and fourth place finish for Delahaye in the 1938 *Vingt-Quatre Heures du Mans*.

The Delahaye 135, bodied in various forms and powered by a variety of 3.5-liter six-cylinder engines, ranging in output from 90 horsepower to more than 150 horsepower, would become one of the most efficient race and rallye cars of its time. On the road, these same chassis would also find acceptance as sports tourers—sports cars pure of spirit and clothed in bodywork as only the French could. The 1946 Cabriolet Narval was perhaps the finest example of the classic French styling idiom; a car of uncommon character, and among the last to come from an automotive culture steeped in prewar traditions that would not survive long into the 1950s.

For Cadillac, 1947 was a pivotal year, marking the last of the great prewar designs, and the last models that would later be considered American Classics.

If you wanted a new Cadillac in 1947, or any American car for that matter, you either knew someone in the business or your name ended up at the bottom of a very long waiting list. There were no discounts, and there was no bargaining. This was car-starved America, five years without a new model in dealer showrooms.

GM design chief Harley Earl, and Cadillac design studio head Bill Mitchell, had made significant styling changes for 1942, the marque's 40th anniversary year, and that gave the GM luxury division a leg up when automobile production resumed after the war. The new models had barely been introduced when production was halted in February 1942. Switching the line back from M-24 Chaffee light tanks to sedans and convertibles was no mean feat, yet it took Cadillac only two months, from August 15, when gasoline rationing officially ended and the War Production Board lifted all restrictions on civilian passenger car production, to early October 1945. Unfortunately, production was hampered by material shortages, particularly sheet steel, and a UAW labor strike.

While designs varied little from prewar cars, revised styling for the 1946 models featured a new grille with six large horizontal bars and new three-piece front and rear bumpers. The most significant restyling was the Cadillac emblem, which was changed to a majestic gold "V" surrounding a Cadillac crest. The new emblem was mounted on both the hood and rear deck lid.

The first postwar models were coupes and sedans, with nearly half of the year's production of 29,194 cars consisting of Series 62 four-door sedans. The stylish Series 62 Convertible Coupe was not introduced until late in the model year, and then only 1,342 came off the Clark Avenue assembly line.

Among prominent model year changes, the striking egg-crate grille design was changed to five vertical bars in 1947 and stamped for the first time instead of die-cast. Another minor but distinctive change was the extension of the top grille bar into the front fenders. At the rear, Cadillac redesigned the emblem once more, this time going to a winged crest on the deck lid. The "V" hood emblem was also changed with the addition of a contoured cloisonné background for the Cadillac crest. The 1947 models were also distinguished by new Cadillac script on the front fenders and bright stainless steel stone shields replacing the black rubber guards used the previous year.

*The interior of the 1946 Figoni Delahaye built for the Aga Khan was very simply detailed. Joseph Figoni chose to use white for the primary color scheme, contrasted by red leather upholstery. The steering wheel and Cotal shifter were also white, as was the instrument panel, smartly accented by two chrome speed lines.*

The Series 62 was Cadillac's best seller, and the Convertible Coupe the most expensive model in the line, priced at $2,902. With production up to capacity, 6,755 Series 62 Convertible Coupes were produced for 1947. The year was again plagued with material shortages and labor union strikes. However, despite setbacks, Cadillac sold 61,926 cars combining the Series 61, Series 62, Fleetwood Sixty Special, and Fleetwood Seventy-Five models. How great was the demand for new Cadillacs? The GM division closed the books on 1947 production in mid-January 1948 with more than 96,000 unfilled orders!

Across town at Packard, the postwar start-up was going poorly. Back in 1942, the all-new Clipper barely had its feet wet when Franklin Delano Roosevelt declared December 7, 1941 "...a date which will live in infamy." In retrospect, the war couldn't have been more damaging to any American auto maker than Packard. The sleek styling of the Clipper was the best that East Grand Boulevard had offered customers since the late 1930s. The basic design was conceived by Dutch Darrin, and what Packard's styling department had planned to do with it throughout the 1940s might well have changed Packard's future. Of course, that's pure speculation. The only hard fact is that on February 9, 1942, after selling more than 30,000 1942 Clippers, Packard joined the rest of the American automotive industry in the war effort and suspended commercial automobile production. Had Packard produced Clippers for the entire 1942 model year, it is estimated that sales would have surpassed 80,000.

*One of the outstanding characteristics of the Henri Chapron design for the 1947 Delahaye 135 MS "Vedette," a word which roughly translates into "movie star," was the use of clear plastic for the steering wheel and all of the controls. The dashboard was burled walnut with a polished chrome fascia around the instruments.*

*The 1947 Delahaye 135 MS Vedette was one of Henri Chapron's finest postwar creations. It is believed that this car was shown on either the Chapron or Delahaye stand at the 1948 Paris Auto Salon. Compared to the 1946 Figoni Delahaye, it is hard to believe they were even designed in the same decade. Such was the diversity of French coachwork. This 135 MS is now part of the Hull & Mullin collection.*

As assembly lines were converted, tooling for the Packard Clippers was covered in Cosmoline, carefully wrapped, and sent to open storage, making way for the production of Merlin aircraft engines and marine engines to be used in PT boats. Throughout the war, the Clipper tooling sat out in the weather, and it wasn't until 1945 that the real damage was realized. As the only remaining model in the Packard line (the rest, tooling and all, having been sold during the war to the Russians), the Clipper's re-launch in 1946 proved to be an exasperating task. It took more than 12 months to get all the machinery cleaned and back into working order. Still, Packard managed to produce 42,102 cars in 1946 for the 1946 and early 1947 model years.

In the summer of 1947, Packard introduced the all-new 1948 Twenty-Second Series, replacing the original Clipper. Packard's new chief stylist, John Reinhart (who would go on to design the Lincoln Continental Mk II for Ford in 1956), remarked that Packard could have continued the Clipper for another two years with minor styling revisions and it would have been a much better-looking car than the 1948 Packard. But the pressure from GM, Ford, and Chrysler, along with new designs from competitive independent auto makers and newcomers like Kaiser-Frazier, was too great. Lamented Reinhart, "All of us at Packard styling wanted to

The 1946 and 1947 Series 62 convertible coupes are ranked among the most collectible of all early postwar Cadillac models for their beautiful pontoon fenders, prominent grille, and handsome styling. The Series 62 was the only convertible model offered and by any standard were the most attractive Cadillacs of the postwar 1940s. This Series 62 convertible is now owned by Noel Thompson.

The luxurious interior of the 1946 and 1947 Cadillac Series 62 allowed comfortable seating for five adults. The sporty convertibles had a base price of $2,902. Hydra-Matic was the most popular option ($186.34), ordered on 92 percent of all 1947 models. The optional Cadillac radio was priced at $73.65.

advance the Clipper design but instead management made a decision to reshape the car entirely." It was a bad decision. The 1948 models launched Packard on the road to ruin while the 1941 through 1947 Clippers became the last Packards recognized as Classics and the first postwar models to achieve Milestone status. They were at once the end and the beginning of an era.

Lincoln was another marque on the road to mediocrity, at least from a Classic perspective. The last remaining trace of the great cars built by Lincoln under Edsel Ford, who died on May 26, 1943, at the age of only 49, was the Continental, which Edsel had designed with Ford stylist Eugene Gregorie in 1940.

Produced through 1942, the Continental was brought back in 1946 with modestly revised styling, and selected as the pace car for the first postwar Indianapolis 500. Minor changes were again made in 1947, and the Continental was withdrawn from the Lincoln lineup in 1948 as Ford Motor Company prepared to introduce its first all-new cars of the postwar era.

By 1949, the Classic car was gone. Never again would any auto maker, foreign or domestic, manufacture automobiles of such extraordinary style and character, nor in such limited numbers as those produced from 1925 to 1948. American and European Classics truly were the world's greatest cars.

The famous Cadillac "V" made its debut on the 1946 and 1947 Cadillac line. Models produced in 1947 featured a contoured cloisonne background behind the Cadillac emblem. Parking or optional fog lamps were incorporated in a panel surrounded by the grille. The fog lamps were an additional $30.12.

It was March 1948, and the end of the line for the Lincoln Continental. On April 22, Ford Motor Company introduced the most extensively changed Lincolns since 1936 (when Lincoln introduced the Zephyr), but in the wake of change there was no place for the prewar-styled Continental. For the final model year, a total of 847 Coupes and 452 Cabriolets rang down the curtain on the last American Classic.

The last throes of French Classic styling, this Delahaye 235M coupe was a prototype bodied by Henri Chapron in 1953 and displayed at the Paris Auto Show. The car was never put into production.

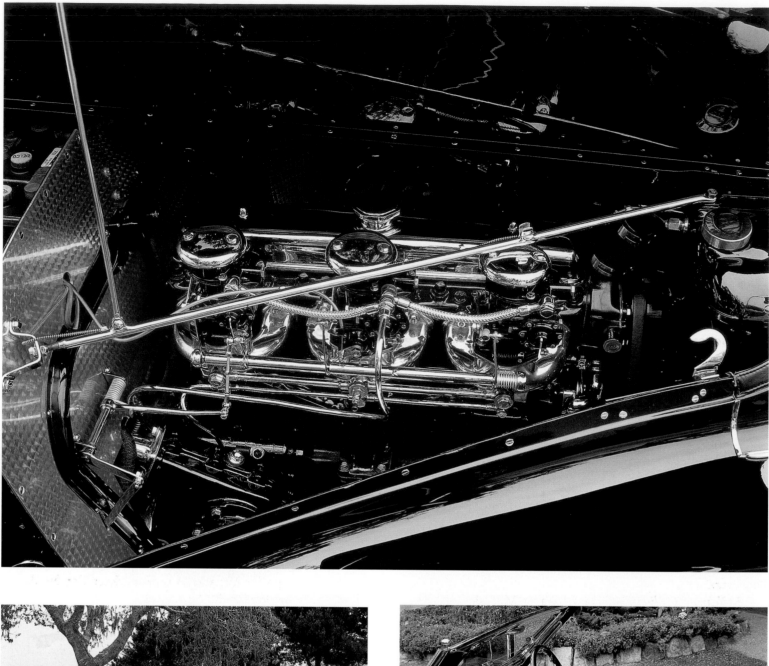

*A later rendition of the Cabriolet Narval by Figoni built in 1948. The use of chrome is more accentuated, as are the fenders and particularly the length of the nose. The interior is perhaps one of the better-styled examples; this car was restored by Craig Jackson with a red leather interior and inserts of dyed ant eater hide. The Delahaye 135M in-line six-cylinder engine produced 160 horsepower.*

# Bibliography

*Standard Catalog of American Cars, 1805-1942*, by Beverly Rae Kimes and Henry Austin Clark, Jr., 1985, Krause Publications.

*Collector Cars*, by Lee Culpepper, 1989, Octopus Books Ltd., London

*The Illustrated Encyclopedia of the World's Automobiles*, by David Burgess Wise, 1979, Quarto Publishing, Chartwell Books, Inc.

*The World Guide to Automobile Manufacturers*, by Nick Baldwin, G.N. Georgano, Michael Sedgwick, and Brian Laban, 1987, Macdonald & Co., London.

*100 Years of the World's Automobiles*, G.N. Georgano, 1962, Floyd Clymer Publications.

*Automobile and Culture*, by Gerald Silk, Henry Flood Robert, Jr., Strother MacMinn, and Angelo Tito Anselmi, 1984, Harry N. Abrams, Inc. N.Y. Publisher.

*Packard—A History of the Motor Car and the Company*, Beverly Rae Kimes, editor, 1978, Automobile Quarterly Publications.

*80 Years of Cadillac LaSalle*, by Walter M.P. McCall, 1982, Crestline Publishing.

*The Marmon Heritage*, by George Philip Hanley and Stacey Pankiw Hanley, 1985, Doyle Hyk Publishing Co., Rochester, Michigan.

*Automobile Quarterly*, Vol. 27, No. 2, Marmon's Masterpieces by Griff Borgeson.

*Marmon —The History of a Success*, published in 1916 by Marmon Sales Extension Division.

*Pace Cars of the Indy 500*, by L. Spencer Riggs, Speed Age Inc.

*The Marmon Post*, published 1920, The Hollenbeck Press.

*Automobile Trade Journal*, August 20, 1920.

*Un Siecle de Carrossiere Francaise*, by Jean-Henri Labourdette, published in French by Edita, 1972. Our special thanks to bookseller T.E. Warth and translator Lisa Seiffert. Portions were also excerpted from Dennis Adler's book, *Mercedes-Benz 110 Years of Excellence*, published in 1996 by Motorbooks International.

*Auburn, Cord, Duesenberg*, by Don Butler, 1992 by Motorbooks International.

*The Cars of Lincoln Mercury*, by Geo. H. Dammann and James K. Wagner, 1987 by Crestline Publishing Co.

*Duesenberg—The Mightiest American Motor Car*, by J.L. Elbert, 1975 by Post-Era Books.

Additional information provided by Jim Hoggett, Indianapolis Motor Speedway Museum, Jack Dunning, the Encyclopedia Americana Vol. 20, 1991 edition, and the World Book Encyclopedia Vol. 14, 1993 edition.

# Index